Help!

For Parents of Teenagers

By Parents for Parents

Volume 6
The Suggestion Circle Series

Edited by

Jean Illsley Clarke,
Sara Monser,
Gail Nordeman, and
Harold Nordeman

1817

Harper & Row, Publishers, San Francisco

Cambridge, Hagerstown, New York, Philadelphia, Washington
London, Mexico City, São Paulo, Singapore, Sydney

*To the hundreds of wise and thoughtful
parents who have shared in this book
some of what they have learned
so that other parents may know that
they are not alone,
they have choices,
and they need not reinvent the wheel.*

The developmental affirmations for children on pages 18 to 22 are adapted from Pamela Levin's therapeutic affirmations in *Becoming the Way We Are* and are used with the permission of the author.

Cover design: Terry Dugan
Illustrations: Jerry Smath

Library of Congress Cataloging-in-Publication Data

Help! for parents of teenagers.

(The Suggestion circle series; vol. 6)
Includes index.
1. Youth—United States. 2. Child rearing—United States. I. Clarke, Jean Illsley. II. Parents for parents. III. Series.
HQ796.H396   1986   649'.125   86-18382
ISBN: 0-86683-456-7

86 87 88 89 90 OPM 10 9 8 7 6 5 4 3 2 1

Contents

CLUSTERS AND SUGGESTION CIRCLES

Appreciations

Thank you, students and foster parents, for your enthusiastic use of Suggestion Circles in our classes and special gatherings. Your rich and wise alternatives excited new thinking in us all.

Thank you, editors, for your clarity, warmth, and productive fun.

Thank you, Chris, Kim, Lindsay, and Kurt, for teaching me as I taught you. And thank you, Carl, for so many years of love and good sense.

—From Sara

My appreciation to Harold for letting his spirit brighten the world and my life, to my children whose growth challenged my own, to my coeditors for their support and knowledge, to all those with whom I've studied, worked, and learned, and to my clients at A Growing Place, Cincinnati, Ohio, and Healdsburg, California.

—From Gail

To my wife, Gail, for being you and for your loving encouragement to grow; to Linda, Donna, Vivian, Barbara, and Joyce, my daughters, for the stimulus to be the father they needed; to my parents, for being there for me; to the coeditors and my colleagues in Transactional Analysis for their knowledge and insights; to all the people in my extended family of clients at A Growing Place and at Healdsburg, and to my contractual sons and daughters everywhere.

—From Harold

My thanks to my own parents for guiding me through successful teenage years and to my children Marc, Jennifer, and Wade for insisting that my husband, Dick, and I do the same with them.

—From Jean

Thanks from all of us to Deane Gradous for conceiving the idea of publishing Suggestion Circles in books. Thanks to Maggie Lawrence for her careful reading and helpful suggestions. Thanks to Dr. Christine Ternand for sharing her medical perspective in writing about abuse and for reading the circles for medical accuracy. Thanks to Mary Ann Lisk, Becky Monson, Vivian Rouson-Gossett, and Nancy Nenovich for their dedication, encouragement, good humor, and typing skills.

—The Editors

Foreword

The teenage years are at once magical and disquieting—for both teenagers and their parents. Erik Erikson tells us that the major growth task facing teens is developing a sense of personal identity. This identity, or sense of self, must be strong and healthy enough to successfully support the teenagers' emerging responsibilities as nurturing and contributing adults. It has also been suggested that a major task of middle age is assisting teenage children to become responsible and happy adults.

The delights of the teen years include the opportunity that both parents and their teenagers have to develop a new, more adult-to-adult relationship. The challenge is to learn how to pace the unfolding of this relationship. We know that teenagers continue to need parental guidance; they also want counsel and support, though they may be reluctant to admit it, even to themselves.

The teen/parent issues that are the subject of the Suggestion Circles in this book are likely to be scattered along the path from adolescence to adulthood. Each issue can be either an obstacle or an opportunity for both parents and their teenagers. If they miss this mutual learning/teaching opportunity, both parents and teens will be cheated.

This is a book for, by, and about parents. It is a testament to the compassion, understanding, and wisdom with which parents can help each other. Most of the all-too-familiar problems facing teens and their parents are discussed here. For parents whose children are entering adolescence, the list of nine potentially difficult areas that appears in the table of contents *could* raise anxiety; the suggestions for coping with them, however, should reduce this anxiety. For each problem, the book's editors present a range of sensible options. These suggestions are wise in themselves, but perhaps their greater value lies in their ability to prompt readers to combine, adapt, and invent ways of coping that more nearly fit the specific situation they face.

This HELP! book, as its editors caution and as its title suggests, is not about the times when things are going smoothly. It is, nevertheless, an optimistic book. Parents will find comfort in the suggestions, which are simple, upbeat, clear, and practical. The writing is warm and friendly, so readers will feel cared for and empowered, not intimidated or demeaned. All this should help parents and their teenagers cope wisely and effectively with the stress that they will inevitably face.

—Dorthea Cudaback, DSW
Cooperative Extension
University of California at Berkeley

What Is This Book About?

This is a book written for parents by parents.

It is a book for the days when you don't know what to do or when what you're doing isn't working. It is *not* a theoretical book about the times when things are going smoothly. It *is* a book of specific, practical suggestions for handling different problems that parents have sought help for in parenting classes around the country.

These parents have attended a class or a group led by a facilitator who is trained in the methods used in the class, "Self-Esteem: A Family Affair." One of these techniques, called the "Suggestion Circle," is used to collect options for parents with problems. Here's how it works: In class, members sit in a circle and listen to a parent describe a problem. Each member of the Circle then offers his or her best suggestion for dealing with it. In this way, the person with the problem benefits from the collective wisdom and experience of the whole group and goes home with a list of suggestions or options.

The Suggestion Circle process is different from brainstorming, which encourages people to offer every idea that comes to mind. It's also different from listening to a teacher or an expert provide "the correct answer." In a Suggestion Circle, *every* answer comes from an "authority," that is, a parent, foster parent, uncle, aunt, or grandparent. And every answer is "correct," since it worked for the person who discovered it, sometimes after many years of experience. The resulting list provides a variety of suggestions and encourages flexibility in the listener or reader. It may suggest a new way of perceiving the problem.

We chose these Circles because they represent problems about which we hear repeatedly in classes or that seem particularly difficult for parents. Leaders collected the suggestions and asked the parents if we could share their responses with you in these books. Each Circle includes the name of the first facilitator or group who sent the problem to us and the location of that class or group. Since similar problems come up in different parts of the country, we have combined suggestions from more than one group.

You will notice that often the answers contradict one another. That needn't bother you; parents and children and homes are different, and what works with one may not work with another or at another time. Use what works for you!

You will find the Suggestion Circles grouped in clusters according to subject matter. We editors have eliminated any ideas that advocated violence because child abuse is illegal and because we do not believe violence helps children. We also eliminated suggestions that implied that parents or children are helpless or that a problem was not serious. We assume that if parents ask for help, the problems are important and serious to them.

We have also written briefly about the characteristic tasks of this stage of *development* and described how parents may *abuse* teens if they misunderstand those tasks. We have given short explanations of *affirmations*, *recycling*, and other topics that are important parts of the "Self-Esteem: A Family Affair" class and are referred to in the Circles.

So here they are, some short reference pieces and eighty-one circles, eighty-one collections of the best ideas from parents who have been there, to you who are there now.

—The Editors

How to Use This Book

You can use this book to help you think. When you want ideas about how to solve a problem, look in the table of contents for a cluster title that seems to include your problem. For example, for the problem of children staying out late, look under "Curfews and Cars and Chores." Or look in the Index for words that describe your problem (like *late*, *coming in late*, or *curfews*) and read about the problems that sound most like yours. Some of the suggestions may not fit your situation or your parenting style. Many of the lists contain contradictions, since there are lots of ways to raise children. Think about which suggestions sound useful for your particular problem.

Reading about what other parents have done will remind you that there are many ways to solve problems and that you can discover and try out new ways that work for you and your child. If you read a list over several times, you will probably find ideas you missed the first time.

Whenever you think of a suggestion that is not listed, write it in your book for future reference. *Our purpose is not to give "one right answer" but to support and stimulate your thinking by offering the wisdom of hundreds of the real child-rearing experts— parents themselves.*

Remember that these suggestions are *not* listed in order of importance—they were offered by a circle of people. If we had printed them in circles, this would be a very big book! We offer them in lists to make a small, convenient book, not to imply that the top suggestion is best.

Use the short sections at the beginning and end of the book as you need them. For a picture of normal adolescent behavior, read **Ages and Stages** and **About Abuse of Adolescents**. You can use that information to think about whether your expectations are reasonable.

The **Affirmations for Growth** section is about healthy messages or beliefs that children this age need to decide are true for them. You can ponder these affirming messages and all the ways, verbal and nonverbal, in which you offer these ideas regularly to your children. Look at **Structuring for Independence and Responsibility** for ways to foster independence by treating these kids as teenagers, not as little children. The section called **Parents Get Another Chance—Recycling** reminds us that our own growth never stops and that we too are doing our own developmental tasks.

If you are distressed about how an older teenager is preparing to leave home, read **Four Ways Young People Leave Home**. There are also directions to follow if you want to lead your own **Suggestion Circle** and suggestions about where to go for additional support.

So read and think. Honor yourself for the many things you do well with your children. Celebrate your growth and the growth of your children. Change when you need to. Remember that your parents did the best they could. You have been doing the best you could. If you want to learn some new ways of parenting, it is never too late to start.

Note: Throughout this book, we have alternated masculine and feminine pronouns; in one section or Circle, the child will be a "she," in the next a "he." In each case, please read "all children."

—The Editors

Ages and Stages

The important tasks of adolescence include integrating the dimension of sexuality into the developmental stages just completed and developing skills in personal relationships. Teens also need to establish support systems beyond the family, decide on a unique personal identity and values, and figure out ways to fit into the adult world.

The completion of these tasks does not progress in a straight line between thirteen and nineteen. Rather, it goes forward in a way that might be visualized as circular. Each circular progression is a recycling process, because it includes reworking the tasks of previous developmental stages as they are reshaped by current experience and the dimension of maturing sexuality. Specific behavior during each teen year reflects the developmental process of this combination of current and recycled developmental tasks. Since some children reach puberty much earlier than others, the ages at which they go through different stages will vary. The following ages are approximations only, and your child may do these tasks on a highly individual timetable.

• Young adolescents, with the new bodies that puberty brings, recycle the need for the sort of *nurturing* given to a newborn: From the self-sufficiency of the rule-governed age of twelve, new teens emerge needing the assurance that there are caregivers willing to provide for their needs, to give them attention, support, and understanding, which they often seek in the form of food, transportation, and clothing. Also, throughout these early teen years, sex is a pervasive topic of thought for adolescents. As these child-persons become maturing sexual-persons, both males and females need parental acceptance of their new sexuality and they also need continued parental nurturing and touching so they can learn that they don't have to use sex to get their touching needs met.

- By late thirteen, if the kids have come to trust that their parent(s) will accept and nurture them as they continue to grow, they will be free to *explore* new experiences—sports, jobs, friends —with energy and enthusiasm. Although these explorations may look directionless, they provide teens with experience and information about their own talents, interests, and relationships to others; and teens will use these explorations to move toward creating their own separate and unique identity.

- With this accumulation of new experiences and feelings to integrate into old beliefs and values, fourteen-year-olds may be forgetful and daydreamy, resistant and negative, and charming and compliant. Beneath this iceberg-tip of confusing behaviors, however, teens experience a growing desire and an ability to *think for themselves*.

- As fifteen-year-olds rework earlier stages in which rules about *power*—especially in relation to the opposite sex—were internalized, they may challenge not only their own old rules but those of parents, friends, and society. In any case, teens will be searching for their own rules and structures. And as they do so, adults in their lives would be wise to give support without feeling unduly resistant, threatened, or rejected. If parents give this support, they will likely thoroughly enjoy the sixteen-year-olds who emerge. As teenagers continue the process of exploration toward individuality, adult respect and support will help them learn to express their needs directly, without resorting to manipulation through personality or sex.

- During the middle or later teenager years, adolescents rework old assumptions and feelings about *who they are* in the light of their new experiences and sexuality. Our teens use those around them, both adults and peers, as models for "trying on" different attitudes, rules, ways of thinking, talking, and relating, in order to discover what feels right for them.

As they move toward competent adulthood, they need to practice *responsibility* for getting their needs met, thinking and expressing their own thoughts and opinions, having their own separate feelings and sharing them, and preparing to leave home to become separate adults in a grown-up world.

What can parents do to help? When we show kids that we feel OK about not having all the answers, we help our children know they can figure out answers for themselves. For example, discovering that we've been using a rule that isn't helpful and choosing to change that rule validates our children in their search for rules that they can make their own. It's important to ask our growing-up children for hugs; it teaches them how to get the touching they need and that it's OK to ask; it also reminds them that everyone needs nurturing touch, that is, touch that has nothing to do with sex. When, as parents, we enjoy being a man or a woman, we assure our kids that it's satisfying to grow from being a boy to a man or girl to a woman. Parental arguments along with visible resolutions help them know that a positive relationship includes disagreements and problem solving as well as joy.

Our children in their teen years will be building on the skills they acquired throughout the years before. As they recycle the developmental stages of those earlier years, they have the chance to expand, rework, and make important decisions about what they've learned about who they are and about how to become responsible, independent adults.

—Sara Monser and Gail Nordeman

Structuring for Responsibility and Independence

The basis of independence and responsibility is adequate internal structure. *All the ways people arrange and organize their thinking, feeling, and behavioral responses make up this structure.* Preteens have developed their structure by gathering information, developing skills, and forming attitudes and beliefs about themselves, others, and the world. Some of these attitudes, conclusions, and beliefs were formed when the children were too young to fully understand what they were choosing.

During adolescence, children are faced with a variety of decisions, and are offered many opportunities to update those early attitudes, conclusions, and beliefs in order to support their growing maturity. This process often creates both internal and external conflict. One of the ways parents help their teens become responsible and independent is by encouraging them to amend and/or update earlier structures.

Responsibility is a learned skill. You do not learn to be responsible and independent all at once; rather you learn to take over and accomplish the tasks of self-care gradually by practicing many skills and by learning through failures and successes. Parents need to encourage teens to make their own choices in safe areas. There are many nonharmful areas—such as dress, hairstyle, music—in which teens can develop their separate identity. If parents attempt to control their teens' behavior in all areas (even those that are safe but not necessarily comfortable for the parents), then teens may resort to more serious activities such as drugs and inappropriate sexual activity to establish themselves as separate from their parents.

Remember, there are many "right" ways to parent teenagers. Keeping in mind that each family is different and each adolescent is unique, you can use the following guidelines, as well as those already mentioned, to create the type of environment that fosters responsibility and independence.

- Visualize your teen as competent and lovable.
- Listen to the thoughts, content, and emotional level of your teen's communication in a nonjudgmental way.
- Challenge through direct communication any beliefs and attitudes your teenager holds that you believe are destructive.
- Recognize, praise, and affirm all positive behaviors and attitudes. Continue to give unconditional love, and support the development of values and morals in all areas.
- Continue to set healthy limits in areas that are potentially dangerous. Limits provide a sense of security as teens practice different ways of being independent.
- Praise what your teen does well, while holding him accountable for what he does poorly. Allow him to experience the consequences, negative or positive, of his behavior.
- Encourage teens to make responsible moral decisions about the expression of their maturing sexuality, as well as about other areas.

- Give permission to and expect your teen to identify and reject destructive messages that invite diminished self-esteem and/or do not help him to be a responsible person.
- Support teens as they search out solutions to problems.

Helping adolescents learn structures for independence and responsibility is a very important gift that parents can give their children. When it seems to parents that they are putting more energy into the parent-teen relationship than the kids are, that is probably true. Think back to your own teenage years and recall the most important thing about any year of your adolescence. Chances are, it was *not* "getting along well with my parents." The children are doing their job, which is to separate. You do yours, which is to continue to provide love, support, and a flexible structure as you separate from them.

—Gail Nordeman

About Abuse of Adolescents

Child abuse and neglect are prevalent and, perhaps, epidemic in our society today. We feel strongly that all children are to be valued and cherished. We believe that children will be better protected when parents know the causes and signs of child abuse and when they learn ways to keep children safe.

Causes of Child Abuse

There are many causes of child abuse. Since this is not a book about the ills of society or emotionally disturbed individuals but about normal, healthy parents and children, we will address only the abuse that springs from parents' misunderstanding of normal growth and development of children at different ages. Sometimes, as children go about their developmental tasks, they do things that are misinterpreted by parents who may be overly severe or hurtful in an attempt to stop or control those normal behaviors. Parents may believe that they are "disciplining," but when they punish their children for doing what is developmentally correct and normal, children are hurt physically or emotionally.

The following behaviors of young people this age are frequently misunderstood:
• Teens are beginning to experiment with ways of expressing their budding sexuality. They have many sexual behaviors and attitudes to explore and decisions to make before they are ready for

sexual intercourse. Unfortunately, many media in our society are reinforcing the fantasy that these children are highly desirable sexual objects. In spite of physical signs of sexual maturity, teens still need the protection of caring adults. It is always sexual abuse when someone misuses a *trust* relationship and gives suggestive kisses or touches a child sexually in any way. The adult is responsible: an adolescent is *never* responsible for the seduction. If there is a difference of more than three years of age between participants, and one participant is a minor, sexual touching is considered rape by law in many states.

• One of the most important tasks of the teenager is to *separate* from the family and become an independent adult. (See **Ages and Stages**.) Many times, teens will escalate negative behaviors as part of this separating task. Caring adults who don't understand this need for separation may become verbally or physically abusive, instead of calmly continuing to set and enforce the important limits.

• As part of the maturing process, teens rework and *upgrade earlier developmental tasks*. (See **Affirmations for Growth**.) The emotional ups and downs that accompany these recycling activities may appear confusing if not understood to be part of normal development. Some adults may become abusive in response to their feeling of confusion.

Signs of Child Abuse

How can you tell if your child has been abused by others? Pay attention to the following:
- A sudden reluctance to wear shorts or bathing suits, which may mean revealing unusual marks around upper thighs.
- Hickey marks on the neck.
- Significant changes in school performance, attitudes, relationships.
- Behavior problems, such as drug abuse, stealing, fire-starting, eating disorders.
- Signs of depression.
- Suicide gestures, such as notes saying "I want to die," attempts to overdose, any forms of self-mutilation.

If you suspect abuse of any kind, find a way to protect your teen. Get help if you need it.

Ways to Help Teens Keep Safe

You protect teens when you do these things:
- Remember that teens need some clear rules, for example, about curfews and car privileges, and they need to have those rules enforced.
- Make certain your teens are capable of staying alone before leaving them alone. Pay special attention to their ability to follow social and safety rules.
- Give them permission to say no to peer pressure.
- Give them permission to call home *anytime* they need help or take a taxi if it's needed for their safety.
- Monitor their driving until they have developed skillful, careful driving habits.

- Become aware of the extent of alcohol abuse and drug abuse in your teens' environment and take action to help your teens protect themselves from that abuse.
- Continue to be a reliable source of information about people and the world. Explain about sexual maturity to your children caringly, lovingly, and knowledgeably, or get a specially trained adult to do it. Information from other sources, such as peers or washroom walls, is often inaccurate or incomplete.
- Help your teens establish a sense of personal responsibility but do not exploit them by expecting them to take major responsibility for household or child care, which are functions of the parents'. You do not allow sports coaches or teachers to exploit them either.

—Christine Ternand, M.D.

Affirmations for Growth

What are affirmations? Affirmations are all the things we do or say that imply that our children are lovable and capable. Belief in these affirmations supports teenagers in their self-acceptance, self-responsibility, and independence and sets the stage for adult developmental tasks.

Here are some special affirming messages that will help young people during their adolescent stage of growth. You give these affirmations by the way you

- interact with your adolescent
- respond to his sometimes dramatic changes in mood and interests as he swings from recycling one stage to another
- admire his emerging sexuality without being seductive
- support his emotional separation first
- support his physical separation later
- (or) support his growing independence while he continues to live at home
- say these affirmations directly in a supportive, loving way

Of course, you have to believe the messages yourself, or they come off as confusing or crazy double messages. If you don't understand or believe an affirmation, don't give that one until you do believe it.

Affirmations for Identity, Separation, and Sexuality

- You can know who you are and learn and practice skills for independence.
- You can learn the difference between sex and nurturing and be responsible for your needs and behavior.
- You can develop your own interests, relationships, and causes.
- You can learn to use old skills in new ways.
- You can grow in your maleness or femaleness and still be dependent at times.
- I look forward to knowing you as an adult.
- My love is always with you, and I trust you to ask for my support.

Once human beings enter a certain developmental stage, they need the affirmations from that stage for the rest of their lives, so teenagers continue to need the affirmations from the earlier stages. (See **Ages and Stages**.) You can offer the affirmations singly or in groups whenever they seem appropriate.

Affirmations for Being

- I'm glad you are alive.
- You belong here.
- What you need is important to me.
- I'm glad you are you.
- You can grow at your own pace.
- You can feel all of your feelings.
- I love you, and I care for you willingly.

Affirmations for Doing

- You can explore and experiment, and I will support and protect you.
- You can use all of your senses when you explore.
- You can do things as many times as you need to.
- You can know what you know.
- You can be interested in everything.
- I like to watch you initiate and grow and learn.
- I love you when you are active and when you are quiet.

Affirmations for Thinking

- I'm glad you are starting to think for yourself.
- It's OK for you to be angry, and I won't let you hurt yourself or others.
- You can say no and push and test limits as much as you need to.
- You can learn to think for yourself, and I will think for myself.
- You can think and feel at the same time.
- You can know what you need and ask for help.
- You can become separate from me, and I will continue to love you.

Affirmations for Identity and Power

- You can explore who you are and find out who other people are.
- You can be powerful and ask for help at the same time.
- You can try out different roles and ways of being powerful.
- You can find out the results of your behavior.
- All of your feelings are OK with me.

- You can learn what is pretend and what is real.
- I love who you are.

Affirmations for Structure

- You can think before you say yes or no and learn from your mistakes.
- You can trust your intuition to help you decide what to do.
- You can find a way of doing things that works for you.
- You can learn the rules that help you live with others.
- You can learn when and how to disagree.
- You can think for yourself and get help instead of staying in distress.
- I love you even when we differ; I love growing with you.

Teenagers who didn't decide to believe these affirmations at younger ages have a wonderful chance to incorporate them during adolescence. If something happened in their lives or in the family that interfered with a decision, or if you, the parent, didn't understand the importance of the developmental tasks, act now. Remember, it is never too late for you to start believing and offering the affirmations.

The affirmations listed here are adapted from the work of Pamela Levin (see **Resources**). You can learn more about how to use these affirmations in families by reading Clarke's *Self-Esteem:*

A Family Affair (see **Resources**). When you discover additional affirmations that your adolescent needs, write them in your book and give them to your teenager.

—The Editors

Parents Get Another Chance—
Recycling

Many parents of adolescents find the teenage years easier than earlier stages. The children are old enough to reason with and are becoming more and more responsible. Other parents, however, are distressed by teenagers' behaviors, interests, values, resistance, and mercurial mood swings.

Some parents of adolescents enjoy the unfolding of the emerging adult and enjoy the "letting go," but others resist the separation and try to maintain control. Almost all parents find the daily demands of nurturing, challenging, and setting limits for adolescents taxing at times. Whatever parents feel when children go through the transition from childhood to adulthood, one of the benefits of this period is that it triggers parents to recycle or to continue working on their own tasks of becoming whole, separate human beings, of owning their sexuality and of expanding their concept of their place in the larger world. Reexamining our own needs for nurturing, exploring, deciding who we are, and what rules we live by can parallel these stages in our adolescents. Parents who "recycle" and re-create better ways to do old tasks along with their kids may make the journey through the teen years a satisfying adventure.

What Is Adult Recycling?

Recycling is the name given to the cyclical growth process that individuals go through, often without noticing it, in which they learn to do important developmental tasks in ever more competent and sophisticated ways. The theory is discussed in Pamela Levin's *Becoming the Way We Are*. Recycling does not mean that we adults regress to a childlike state, but rather that our life experiences demand that we continually develop more skillful ways of doing developmental tasks. Besides having a natural rhythm of our own, we parents often recycle or upgrade the tasks typical of the stages our children are in. I have talked with hundreds of parents about this idea. Many of them have reported, often with some surprise, that they *are* working on some of the same tasks as their children. They are expanding their values, exploring new aspects of their sex roles, and finishing old separations. It is a normal, healthy, and hopeful aspect of living with growing children.

Affirmations for Growth

The affirmations that are helpful to our children are also healthy for us. (See page 18.) If we didn't get the affirmations we needed the first time around (and many of us didn't), we can think how they fit for us and accept them now as we offer them to our children.

—Jean Illsley Clarke

A. School

My teenager is failing a class. He is not concerned but I am. What can I do?

- This child may need to fail and take the consequences to get the message that he is responsible for his school work.
- Find out why he is not interested. Ask him to think if he can make the course interesting for himself.
- Arrange a meeting with the teacher for your son and you.
- Ask him what he plans to do about it.
- Check to see if this is solely his problem or if it is part of a larger family problem, such as grief, divorce, or alcoholism.
- Give him a choice. Take a privilege away if he doesn't raise his grade. Decide on a reward for improvement.
- Consider moving him to a teacher or school that will expect more of him or be more suited to his needs.
- Give him lots of recognition for who he is aside from this problem.
- Remember your worth is not determined by his grades.
- Have his hearing tested. Some children who can't hear pretend they don't care about grades.

(See also D-1, E-2, F-2, F-6, and **Structuring for Independence and Responsibility**.)

Thanks to Suzanne Morgan, Circle from Albert Lea, Minnesota

My fifteen-year-old daughter came home with two "D"s and four "C"s. She is capable of "B"s and wants to go to college. How do I encourage her to believe in herself and to improve her grades?

- Let her know you will always love her and that grades are for her, not you.
- Brainstorm with her ways she can bring her grades up and how you can help if she needs it.
- Be available to listen.
- Celebrate each grade she brings up.
- Be sure women have permission and encouragement to be smart in your family, even if that means she is smarter than her boyfriend.
- If poor grades are a part of a bigger problem, like depression, ask her to go with you to a school counselor. Be sure she knows what grade level she needs to get into college.
- Help her make a study schedule, if she wants your help. Eliminate distractions—radio, TV, phone calls, etc., during study times.
- Get a tutor for her.
- Check on drugs and sexual activity. Confront her if you find a problem.
- Help her develop a peer study group.
- Ask her if her friends are supporting her wish to go to college. She may need some new friends.

(See also F-1 and **Ages and Stages, Affirmations for Growth**.)

Thanks to Roxy Chuchna, Circle from Albert Lea, Minnesota

Our daughter will not get involved in school activities. What can I do?

- Provide opportunities for her to join other groups besides those at school, for example, Y, civic center groups, church groups, hospital aide, Search and Rescue team, etc.
- Trust her to know what is best for her.
- Invite her to bring her friends to the house. Casually ask about their school activities. Find out how their parents view their activities.
- Look at the possibility that some children are not interested in school activities and do just fine in the business world and adult life.
- Check out your motives. Let her be who she is. Give her the freedom to be herself.
- Go to some mother-daughter or father-daughter events with her.
- Look at her friends. What are their interests?
- Explain how school activities will benefit her in the future—job resume, college applications, etc.
- Is she in some other group activities? If not, tell her you want her to find one activity, in or out of school, to participate in.
- If the girl is a real loner, consider some counseling.

(See also **Affirmations for Growth.**)

Thanks to Nat Houtz, Circle from Seattle, Washington

My athletic child is being pushed by his coach to do and achieve more and more at sports. I'm not sure what to do, if anything.

- Look at whether sports are interfering with his growth as a well-rounded person. If so, decide with him how to achieve a healthy balance.
- There are limits on this. You and your son decide what they are. Limit the coach if you have to.
- Be aware that coaches can sometimes influence even academic grades in order to keep an athlete playing. This teaches manipulation and dishonesty while cheating a student of a sound education.
- Discuss with your child the degree to which he minds being pushed and what he would like you to do to help him out.
- Watch carefully that he doesn't hide injuries from you in order to keep on playing.
- During this time give lots of strokes for Being. "I love you whether you play or not."
- Discuss the pros and cons of playing a sport with your child. Allow him to make his own decision, and support him.
- Ask your son, "Are your sports fun? Do *you* like playing?"

(See also **Ages and Stages** and **Affirmations for Growth**.)

Thanks to Sara Monser, Circle from Lafayette, California

One teacher at school is giving my daughter a hard time. What do I do about it?

- Set up a parent-teacher-student conference. If that doesn't work, get a counselor involved.
- Ask the child, "What specifically is bothering you about what the teacher does?"
- During the conference, have the teacher define his or her view of the problem and then decide what to do.
- If the conference doesn't work, support your child in moving into another class.
- Let your child know that you support her in her decision about handling this situation.
- Look at the history of both teacher and child. Is this a teacher many children have trouble with? If so, get your child moved to another teacher, and start action to protect other children. Or does your child have trouble with lots of teachers? If so, get counseling for her.
- Say, "I love you, and I will help you in whatever way you need me in order to work this out."
- Talk to the school counselor to see if you can get additional information or help there.
- Figure out with your daughter what can be done; then help her do it.
- See the teacher, without your child, and take your spouse.

Thanks to Sara Monser, Circle from Lafayette, California

My fifteen-year-old is a truant from high school and lies about it.

• Find out why he is missing school, give him family consequences and confront the lies with facts.
• Involve a third party such as a school or family counselor in a discussion of the problem.
• Ask him what he plans to do about the future and this problem.
• Tell him he is important and it's important for you to understand why he's truant and why he lies.
• Tell him what the consequences will be if he's truant or lies again. Carry through.
• Tell him you will ask the school to call you if he is late or absent.
• Expect honesty and figure out if you have been punishing honesty.
• Share your concern with your other children and see if they know what's going on with the child.
• Ask him about his goals for his life and how education fits into his achieving those goals.
• Look for ways you can get involved at school.
• Ask him what happens to people who are truant and lie when they are twenty and twenty-five.
• Consider the possibility of drug abuse by him or someone in the family system.

(See also C-4, C-5, C-9, and D-1.)

Thanks to Jean Clarke, Circle from Minnetonka, Minnesota

We are moving to a different town. My sixteen-year-old child is scared and acting out. What can we do?

- Give her a lot of love. Make sure she knows what's going to happen next.
- Invite a friend of hers to come and spend a week or two with you after you move.
- Provide as much certainty as possible in her life.
- Take your daughter along when you go to look for a new home and to visit the schools.
- Sit down as a family and talk about how each person feels about the move.
- Contact someone in the new area who has a child the same age as your child. Introduce them.
- She didn't make the decision to move. Help her identify all the things she can make decisions about.
- Say, "Honey, I'm scared, too. Let's make a list together of sixteen ways you and I can help each other get past our fears." Read the chapter on support groups in *Self-Esteem: A Family Affair*. (See **Resources**.)
- If she is in a good school and social situation, consider finding a family for her to live with while she finishes the school year.

(See also **Ages and Stages, Affirmations for Growth,** and **Parents Get Another Chance— Recycling**.)

Thanks to Samara Kemp, Circle from Modesto, California

B. Drugs, Sex, and Health

How do I say no to my child who wants to go to a party where alcohol and drugs will be used?

• Say no and offer another option, such as having friends at your house.

• Say no onto a tape recorder. Listen to the tone of your voice to see if you might be inviting your child to argue.

• Stand in front of your mirror and practice saying no in different body positions and tones of voice. Don't smile when you say it to her.

• Gather other parents and friends together to support you. Practice with each other.

• Say, "Because I trust you, saying no is hard for me. Because I care, 'no' it is."

• Figure out what makes it so difficult for you to say no.

• Look up "no" in six different languages. Use them all!

• Practice saying no in other areas of your life.

• Use your vocal cords and say, no!

• If your child is underage say, "No. It is against the law for you to consume alcohol. Drugs are illegal."

(See also B-2, B-3.)

Thanks to Sara Monser, Circle from Concord, California

What kind of rules should I set for my sixteen-year-old daughter regarding drinking and driving?

• If she drinks at a party, set a rule that she is to call home for a ride.
• Make an absolute rule about no drinking and driving.
• Listen to her feelings about drinking and stay firm on your rule that drinking is not permitted until she is of legal age.
• Say, "If you drink, I will take away your privileges." Let her know you'll provide a ride home if for any reason she will be unsafe in a car.
• Have her call you or a sober friend for a ride if anyone is drinking and driving.
• Say, "Drinking for children underage is illegal. You may not drink alcoholic beverages."
• Each of you sign a contract stating that neither of you will drink if you must drive.
• Think about what rules you feel are appropriate for a child in your family, then state them clearly to her and enforce them.
• Read *Steering Clear: Helping Your Child Through the High-Risk Drug Years* by Cretcher. (See **Resources**.)
• "If you drink, don't drive."
• If you drink when you have the car you are grounded for three months.

(See also B-1.)

Thanks to Sara Monser, Circle from Lafayette, California

I think my seventeen-year-old is drinking too much. What can I do?

- Say, "Stop! Drinking is against the law at your age. You must not drink."
- Get him evaluated immediately by a substance-abuse agency.
- Recount to him specific actions that have caused you to become concerned. You are the parent. Set rules and consequences.
- Think about whether there is anything you do that encourages him to drink, such as covering for him.
- Read *An Elephant in the Living Room* by Marion Typpo and Jill Hastings. It talks about how to cut through denial. (See **Resources**.)
- Get in touch with Alcoholics Anonymous, the Hot Line in your city or the National Council on Alcoholism.
- Call your local alcohol treatment center for information and actual help with confronting his behavior.
- Tell him that young people develop cirrhosis of the liver, which is eventually fatal, from drinking an amount of alcohol much smaller than that which affects adults, and that the disease progresses faster than in adults.

(See also B-1, D-1, and **Where to Go for Additional Support**.)

Thanks to Harold Nordeman, Circle from Cincinnati, Ohio

I just learned that my nineteen-year-old niece, who had been through alcohol treatment, has started drinking again. What can I do to help?

- Go to her, tell her what you have heard, and ask her if it is true. Ask if there is anything you can do to help.
- Call your sister-in-law and brother and offer to be a support to them if they will tell you what they need.
- Let your brother know you love him, and that you know about his daughter's drinking again.
- Suggest a qualified assessment to find out the degree of her abuse.
- See a film on alcoholism. Learn all you can. Take action on the information.
- Attend an Al-Anon meeting tonight.
- Get information on drug abuse. Confront; don't gloss over it.
- Invite your brother and sister-in-law to go to an Al- Anon meeting with you.
- Learn about alcoholism and see if you are contributing to the problem in any way.
- Evaluate your relationship with her. Do whatever you can to help support her sobriety.
- Tell her how you are feeling, and invite her to share her feelings.

(See also B-3 and **Where to Go for Additional Support**.)

Thanks to Carole Gesme, Circle from Minneapolis, Minnesota

I think my teenagers may be using drugs. What are some clues? How can I find out about it?

- Ask them.
- Go to community programs that offer information on drugs. Your local alcohol council may have information, files, handouts, etc.
- Observe what kind of friends they are hanging around with. That is often a telling clue.
- Look for sudden changes in mood or behavior, or for school problems.
- If they are evasive and reclusive, that may be a clue that they are using drugs.
- If your kids have more problems in general than they usually have, that may be a clue.
- Red eyes, changes in pupil size, appetite, sleep patterns, and grooming are frequent clues.
- Do they look as if they crawled out from under a rock?
- Refusal to discuss things with you may be a clue.
- Read *Not My Kid* by Polson and Newton or *Getting Tough on Gateway Drugs: A Guide for the Family* by DuPont. (See **Resources**.)

(See also B-6 and **Where to Go for Additional Support**.)

Thanks to Carol Gesme, Circle from Minneapolis, Minnesota

My child is smoking pot. What shall I do?

- Be prepared to enforce anything you say you will do.
- Get the support of other parents.
- Contact the local law enforcement agency to find out the law in your community.
- Tell him to stop.
- Ask him what he gets out of it and suggest that he find healthy highs like running or getting involved in an exciting hobby or activity. Back him all the way.
- Get an evaluation by a drug-abuse agency.
- Try therapy.
- Say, "Stop." Put a time limit on it and if he hasn't stopped by that time he goes into treatment.
- Have him talk to a peer who is recovering from chemical dependency.
- Separate the behavior from the person. Tell him that you love him and he has to stop smoking dope.
- Have him attend Narcotics Anonymous meetings.
- Write to the National Institute on Drug Abuse for *Parents: What Can You Do About Drug Abuse?*. (See **Resources**.)

(See also B-1, B-5, D-1, and **Where to Go for Additional Support**.)

Thanks to Julia Moen, Circle from Minneapolis, Minnesota

My son wants to have his girlfriend in his room with him "to listen to records." What should I do?

• Tell him to keep the door open.
• Tell them OK and you will bring some snacks up to them. Then do it and continue to look in on them frequently.
• Say, "Bring your records down to the family room."
• Say, "No, it is inappropriate in our home for a young man to have a young woman in his room."
• Tell him, "Yes, it's OK, as long as you will keep it friendly and not sexual."
• Figure how to set up another space in the house for them and respect their privacy.
• Set a limit on the amount of time they can spend alone in the bedroom.
• Explain that the bedroom has sexual implications for couples who are attracted to each other. Don't let him do it.
• Find out why the bedroom is so important to him. If you feel convinced the reasons are valid, and he can handle the situation competently, consider allowing it.

(See also B-12, D-1.)

Thanks to Gail Nordeman, Circle from Cincinnati, Ohio

My daughter and her boyfriend can't keep their hands off each other. She is only fourteen. What can I do?

- It sounds like she needs limits. Say, "All this touching is not appropriate for someone your age. Do you need to stop seeing this boy, or can you keep your touching within safe limits?"
- Read Ruth Bell's *Changing Bodies, Changing Lives* or Peter Mayle's *What's Happening to Me?* with her. (See **Resources**.)
- Find out if she is doing what her boyfriend wants just to please him because she's afraid of losing him.
- Accept her excitement, then help her set limits and find other things to do with her boyfriend.
- Move.
- Make sure you discuss with her the consequences of intercourse: babies, abortions, feeling loved, commitment, disappointment, and venereal disease.
- Are they having intercourse? If they are, take action to get it stopped. She is too young for this. The loss of innocence can affect them the rest of their lives.
- Talk with her about the difference between nurturing touch and sexual touch. Increase the amount of nurturing touch you are offering her.

(See also B-9, D-1, D-6, **Ages and Stages,** and **Structuring for Independence and Responsibility**.)

Thanks to Sara Monser, Circle from Lafayette, California

I think my teenager may be sexually active. We've never talked about sex at all. How do I initiate talks about birth control, social problems, and diseases?

- Say, "Please read *Teenage Body Book* by McCoy and Wibbelsman or *Changing Bodies, Changing Lives* by Ruth Bell. In a few days, I'll be asking what you think of the contents." (See **Resources**.)
- Relate past experiences of your own and share the values you've chosen because of them.
- Give him *The Facts of Love* by Alex and Jane Comfort. Talk about it later. (See **Resources**.)
- Listen to how he's feeling without criticizing.
- Ask him, "What place do you think sex has in a love relationship?"
- Start now. Talk about sex, love, bonding, marriage, and commitment.
- Tell him you are concerned.
- Ask him what sex means to him—socially, physically, emotionally—and discuss the possible consequences.
- Be comfortable with your own sexuality, so you can talk with him, and he with you.

(See also B-8, D-1, E-1, E-3, **Ages and Stages**, and **Structuring for Independence and Responsibility**.)

Thanks to Sara Monser, Circle from Concord, California

I found birth control pills in my fourteen-year-old daughter's room. What should I do?

- Find out if she is using them or not and if she is having intercourse or not.
- Tell her you love her and are concerned.
- Tell her she's too young emotionally to have intercourse.
- Take action! Get help.
- Remind her that her body is hers and is not to be used to please someone else.
- Look with her at statistics on effects of the pill on a young body, the relation of cervical cancer to early intercourse, ineffectiveness of the pill, and the prevalence of diseases.
- Look to see if the limits and rules at your house are over-rigid or too loose. *You* set the standards.
- Get help from a family counselor.
- Look for the possibility of too little nurturing touch at your house or the possibility of sexual molesting. Get counseling.
- Talk to her about the role of intercourse in a committed love relationship and that she is too young for this.
- Give her *What's Happening to My Body?* by Madaras. You read *Talking with Your Teenager* by Bell and Zeiger. (See **Resources**).

(See also B-9, D-1, **Ages and Stages**, and **Affirmations for Growth**.)

Thanks to Sara Monser, Circle from Lafayette, California

I found my seventeen-year-old daughter's birth control pills. What should I say?

• Say, "I found your birth control pills. Let's talk."
• Affirm her responsibility in taking precautions, then ask about her plans for a career, marriage, and motherhood.
• Look at your daughter's relationships. Discuss lovingly possible effects on her, including disease, pregnancy, her reputation, her own image of herself, and the long-term effects of abortion.
• Tell her how you feel and what your hopes are.
• Set your limits while she is living with you.
• Let her know you love her.
• Emphasize that the choice of sharing her body in intercourse is hers and to be done *only* for her reasons and values, not in response to someone else's wishes or to peer pressure.
• Assure her that even though she has had sex, she does not have to say yes again if she chooses not to.
• Have her read *Our Bodies, Ourselves* by the Boston Women's Health Book Collective and *The Facts of Love* by Alex and Jane Comfort. (See **Resources**.)

(See also B-10, D-1, **Ages and Stages**, and **Structuring for Independence and Responsibility**.)

Thanks to Gail Nordeman, Circle from Cincinnati, Ohio

I know my nineteen-year-old son is sleeping with his girlfriend, but I'm uncomfortable with their sharing a room when they're in my home.

• Say, "No way in our house."
• Make clear to them your values didn't change, and they must respect your values in your house.
• Decide what you can tolerate and be consistent with your own values; then enforce rules to support your values.
• Tell them if they can't abide by your rules in your home, they must stay someplace else.
• Prepare a room for each and if they bring up the issue of sleeping together, explain that you do not support their behavior.
• Tell your son, "I love you, and I'm uncomfortable with your sleeping in the same room. I want you to find a way to honor my values."
• Say, "You are not married, and you may not sleep in the same room in my home."
• Insist that the friend sleep at someone else's house when your son is home.
• Decide if and when it will be OK, and then tell them your decision and what you expect from them in the meantime.

(See also B-1, B-7, C-14, and D-1.)

Thanks to Sara Monser, Circle from Lafayette, California

My daughter is pregnant. I am against abortion, but a baby now will destroy the life we've hoped for her. Help me think about it.

- Get good prenatal care for her and see that all possibilities for a good adoptive home are investigated.
- Be aware that pregnancy can be very dangerous for a young person whose body is not mature enough to handle it.
- Consider whether abortion, as negative as it may be, might be less harmful than the other options available.
- Your daughter's wishes must be taken into account as well as yours.
- Look at what will happen to you, your child, your family, and the baby if the pregnancy goes to term.
- Have a conference with the father of the child and his family before any decision is made.
- Keep in mind that every child needs two parents and deserves to be wanted and to be raised in a whole family by loving parents. What is your daughter ready for?
- There is no quick fix. Give your daughter support in every possible way. State your views without blaming and both of you get help and counsel.
- Your daughter has some hard choices to make. Help her all you can.

(See also D-1, I-4, and **Ages and Stages**.)

Thanks to Sara Monser, Lafayette, California

My daughter is so thin I'm afraid she's anorexic. What should I do?

- Take her to her doctor for a physical to see if her weight is within normal range for her age and height.
- Look in the phone book for an eating disorders clinic. Make an appointment for an evaluation. Now!
- Share with her your concern and figure out together what each of you can do.
- Tell her you love her.
- Monitor her eating habits. Look for diet pills, laxatives, diuretics, or other drugs. Notice whether she is exercising compulsively and if her menstrual periods have stopped. Ask your doctor for help.
- Get help from people who know about anorexia.
- Affirm her as a woman and let her know it's OK for her to grow up.
- Ask her how she sees herself and discuss how women are portrayed in the media.
- Decide if you may be expecting perfection from her. If so, take the pressure off. Love her as she is, warts and all.
- If she is anorexic, recognize the suicidal aspect of her behavior. Ask her to make a commitment to live. Get help.
- Read Steven Levenkron's *The Best Little Girl in the World* or other books on anorexia. (See **Resources**.)

Thanks to Gail Nordeman, Circle from Cincinnati, Ohio

My daughter was raped. I don't know what to do to help her.

- Tell her that you love her and look for expert help for her, yourself, and your family.
- Call your minister, family physician, and the Rape Crisis Center for help.
- Accept the situation—no denial. Don't blame her. Let her know you love and honor her. Then call whoever you need to get counsel and help.
- Ask her how she feels about it and accept all of her feelings. She may need to talk about it many times, and you may too.
- Take immediate action—take her to the hospital. Call the police. Decide later if you want to prosecute.
- She may be feeling guilty. She is not to blame. Learn about victim blame and guard carefully against it.
- Make sure she knows this was a crime of sexual violence and the attacker bears the entire blame.
- Release any excess anger with a counselor, not against any member of your family. Use your anger to think and resolve the problem.
- It is important for her to separate this violent sexual act from her own sexuality. Make clear to her that this was misuse of power.
- Read *If She Is Raped* by McVoy and Brookings. (See **Resources**.)

Thanks to Harold Nordeman, Circle from Cincinnati, Ohio

C. Parent and Teen Relationships

What do I do when my child won't answer my questions?

- Write your question on paper and hand it to him. Tell him you need an answer.
- Say, "Look at me. Stop what you are doing for two minutes and respond to my questions."
- Take him to an ear doctor. He may have a hearing problem.
- Don't ask him if he will do something if you won't accept no for an answer. Just tell him to do it.
- Go to a communication class and examine your words, tone, and gestures.
- Stand in front of him. Hold his shoulders and tell him that you are important and deserve to have an answer; then ask again.
- Say, "No answer, no weekend privileges."
- Did the secretiveness start suddenly? Have you considered that he may be on drugs?
- Look at the way you answer questions. How do you model giving answers to people in your family?
- Examine your questions. Maybe they are too intrusive.
- Turn the question into a direction or a wish.

(See also C-4, C-5, D-1, J-4.)

Thanks to Deane Gradous, Circle from St. Paul, Minnesota

My thirteen-year-old wants to take over as parent. What can I do?

- Have a family meeting and define roles.
- Say, "I appreciate good thinking, but *I* will do the parenting."
- Say, "You don't need to take care of me."
- Say, "Thanks for the offer, but I'll keep my job as parent."
- Ask the child questions about what caretaker jobs each of you will be responsible for.
- Talk about responsible roles for different ages of people.
- If she wants a pet, buy her one.
- Look for a variety of ways to express love. You retain the parent role.
- Examine your own behavior to see if there are ways in which you are unconsciously asking your child to take care of you.
- Let your child take over some tasks that support the whole family, like meal planning or shopping or keeping one room clean.
- Set aside ten minutes a day for your child to give family members "parent" suggestions and criticisms. That is all.

(See also J-1 and **Parents Get Another Chance— Recycling**.)

Thanks to Darlene Montz, Circle from Yakima, Washington

How can I deal with a thirteen-year-old who has become very sassy and critical?

- While you tell her your feelings about her sassiness, remember how important it is for thirteen-year-olds to get lots of love and Being messages. (See p. 18.)
- Charge her a fee each time she is sassy.
- Ask her to think of ways she can respond differently.
- Tell her you intend to treat her respectfully and expect her to treat you the same way.
- Catch her being pleasant and compliment her.
- Remember that this may be temporary and due to hormonal changes.
- Don't sass her back.
- When she sasses say, "Stop, start over and say something kind." If she doesn't, do not respond in any way.
- Say, "Ouch, that hurts!"
- Have her do something for you, such as get you a cup of coffee, give a shoulder rub, etc., each time she is sassy!
- Restate what she says in a clear, kind way. Ask her if that was what she meant to say.

(See also D-1, D-4, **Ages and Stages**, and **Parents Get Another Chance—Recycling**.)

Thanks to Betty Beach, Circle from Plymouth, Minnesota

How can I let my son know how I feel when I find out he has kept secrets of things I need to know or that he has lied to me? I want him to trust me.

- Say, "I found out this went on and I feel left out. Next time I want to find out from *you* what happened, not in a roundabout way."
- Figure out with him a code word that tells him in public that you need more information so he can tell you at the first opportunity.
- Say, "Look here, I feel (angry, sad, worried). I don't have all the information and I feel mistrusted. Will you tell me what happened?"
- Don't beat around the bush. Express your frustration and expect accurate information. Find out why he doesn't trust you.
- Say, "In order to be a good parent to you, I need to know certain things. When I don't get that information I feel scared and helpless."
- Say, "Perhaps if I had known, I could have helped."
- Ask, "Have I been worthy of your trust in the past?" If he says no, ask, "How can I earn that trust again?"
- Say, "It's OK for you to keep secrets to yourself for your own privacy. If you want to talk to me about them, I'll be available. It's not OK to lie."
- Make the consequences fit the lie.

(See also C-1, D-1, and J-4.)

Thanks to Ellen Peterson, Circle from Lafayette, California

What can I do to build a better relationship with a manipulative teen?

- When she is not manipulative, respond positively.
- Get a clear picture of how you have been a part of the problem and change your part of it.
- Tell her directly that you are working to build a better relationship with her.
- She learned how to manipulate. Now she can learn how to get what she wants in a straightforward way. Be careful not to respond positively or to laugh or to brag about her tricks.
- Find a therapist for you both together or separately to work on the relationship.
- Tell her that her manipulation is not OK and that you expect her to change.
- Clear up any tendency *you* have to manipulate.
- Take a parenting class to learn some new options.
- When you realize you have been manipulated, complain—rain on her. Don't hide it. Let her know how her behavior affects others.
- Rollo May says in *Power and Innocence* that manipulative power is power over another person and may have originally been invited by the other person's own desperation or anxiety. (See **Resources**.)

(See also C-1, C-9, D-1, J-5, and **Structuring for Independence and Responsibility**.)

Thanks to Judi Salts, Circle from Yakima, Washington

What do I do when my teen says, "Don't act mushy in front of my friends" and doesn't want me to touch him?

• Ask what "mushy" means and how he wants you to act in front of people.
• Do any public touching only when clowning around and having fun.
• Watch for opportunities when you're alone to offer a backrub. Pat him on the back for a "good job" and such.
• Practice appropriate touching in all relationships—with family and with friends. Show him in this way that touching is OK.
• Respect his request in public and ask before hugging or touching in private.
• Talk about the difference between nurturing touches and sexual touches.
• Celebrate that he is in this stage of development. My boys went through it and it didn't last long.
• Joke about it when his friends aren't around. Call after the kid, "Darn! You got away without a hug again!"
• Say, "Even though I would like to hug you, your touching needs are important, too!"
• Don't touch him. Say, "I respect your space. When you are ready for a hug or pat let me know."

(See also J-3, **Ages and Stages**, and **Affirmations for Growth**.)

Thanks to Ellen Peterson, Circle from Lafayette, California

Do you have developmental information and suggestions for responding to a fourteen-year-old daughter's accusations that her parents don't love her?

- Kids who are becoming separate from their parents often convince themselves their parents are awful.
- Say, "I do love you. Even if you don't believe it right now, I do love you."
- If she is sad about giving up dependence and scared of being independent, she may be showing that by accusing you of not caring.
- Think of ways to give her more . . . or fewer . . . chances to be independent of you, whichever you think she needs.
- Intimacy and separation can sometimes be helped by friendly hassling in a way that invites both people to feel good about themselves. (Clarke's *Self-Esteem: A Family Affair* discusses hassling. See **Resources**.)
- Make her a three-foot card in the shape of a heart and write "I love you" on it. Give it to her.
- Discuss with her how she thinks parents who love their fourteen-year-olds should behave. Compare her beliefs with yours.

(See also C-6, J-7, **Ages and Stages**, and **Affirmations for Growth**.)

Thanks to Jean Clarke, Circle from Minneapolis, Minnesota

What do I say when my children say, "You don't trust me" about school work and about their social life?

- Explain that trust is earned by being honest and responsible.
- Clarify that rules are designed for their safety and well-being and to minimize negative influences.
- Point out that the issue may not be one of trust, but of not subjecting them to volatile situations they may not yet have the maturity or experience to cope with.
- If the child has actually been untrustworthy, tell him what he must do to rebuild the broken trust.
- Be sure to provide a consistent role model of trustworthiness. Do what you say you will do.
- Say, "We trust you as long as you are trustworthy. If you break that trust, you must regain it by the way you behave."
- Tell him your job is to gradually shift more responsibility to him, and ask him if he is ready for some more.
- Point out that trusting himself to behave consistently with his own goals is the most important kind of trust.
- If you don't trust him, say, "Correct. I don't trust you today. But I will as soon as you show me by your behavior that you deserve it."

(See also C-1, C-7, D-1, and J-4.)

Thanks to Sara Monser, Circle from Lafayette, California

My fifteen-year-old daughter has run away for short periods three times. She comes home on her own. What should I do?

• Find out what community resources are available to help you with the problem.

• Spend extra, special time with her.

• Say, "Stay here and work this out with us. People learn how to get along in their families. We can help or we will get help."

• Tell her that you love her and that her behavior is not acceptable.

• Find a counselor for her, alone or in a group.

• Get therapy for the family as a whole.

• Say, "This must stop immediately." Then take clear, positive action. Get school teachers and counselors to help in supporting your efforts, whatever you decide to do.

• Say, "You are still my responsibility; if you run away again, I will call the police."

• When she needs some space, arrange for her to stay with another family for a few days while your family continues to work on a resolution to the problem.

• Figure out with her what she's running away from or to. Brainstorm with her about possible solutions.

• Say, "I feel like running away at times, too, but I don't. We'll get help."

(See also **Where to Go for Additional Support.**)

Thanks to Sara Monser, Circle from Concord, California

My kids won't participate in family activities. How should I handle this?

- Allow choices based on development. (Must the fourteen-year-old do it because the nine-year-old must?)
- Insist on participation for significant events and give the kids a choice on other occasions.
- Talk with your children about how to maintain involvement with the family while they continue to grow and prepare to go out into the world.
- If your teens don't want to eat meals with you, together choose two times during the week when the whole family will eat together.
- Include kids in the planning of family events and outings. Sometimes do what they want to do.
- Tell them, "It's OK if you don't participate sometimes."
- Spend some individual time with each child as well as family time.
- Begin to develop new interests of your own.
- Watch the interaction during family activity. If kids are being treated like second-class citizens, change that.
- As children mature, *invite* their participation because you enjoy their company and contribution rather than *demand* it as a duty.

(See also D-1, D-6, E-2, and **Ages and Stages**.)

Thanks to Maggie Lawrence, Circle from Seattle, Washington

My daughter's grades are OK, but she works six hours every day in addition to school, so we never see her. What can I do?

• Talk to her about why she works six hours a day.
• Offer some financial help if you can.
• Tell her you miss seeing her and arrange some time together each week.
• Arrange your schedule so you can be there when she is home.
• Think of creative ways to let her know you love her and miss her, such as making her special foods, leaving little notes, sewing something for her, etc.
• Plan together to go on an outing.
• Look at what you want or need from your daughter and what other sources you have for getting that need met.
• Ask your daughter, "What do you need from me at this time in your development?" Figure out what you will do.
• Offer her a backrub before she goes to bed. Allow time afterwards for conversation with her if you are both still awake.

(See also **Ages and Stages**.)

Thanks to Judy Popp, Circle from Yakima, Washington

What do I do or say to my angry thirteen-year-old adopted son, who wants to meet his natural mother?

- I am adopted. I found my family when I was twenty-five. I think a thirteen-year-old needs to be reassured that you won't send him back. I worried about it from thirteen to sixteen. Don't begin the search until early adulthood. Say, "I am your parent, and I will love you forever."
- Help him express his feelings by listening carefully and without judging.
- If he hasn't heard the story of his adoption and wants to know, tell him.
- Tell him you will make every effort to let him know his mom when he is grown up.
- Give him a picture or memento of her if you can.
- Suggest that he write down all the things he wants to say to her. Ask him to save the paper and add to it whenever he wants to.
- Say, "I know the name of the worker who placed you. We will ask for advice."
- Ask him if he wants to write a letter about himself to place in his mother's file. She may be waiting until he grows up to contact him.
- Read Vera Fahlberg's book *Attachment and Separation* for information on bonding and testing (See **Resources**.)

(See also G-5.)

Thanks to Shirley Bullock, Circle from Spring Lake Park, Minnesota

My fifteen-year-old daughter will not speak or look directly at her stepfather of a year unless the situation absolutely requires it. How can I work with my daughter so she will at least be respectful?

• Tell her how you feel about her behavior and specifically what you want her to do.
• Maybe she really doesn't respect him. Ask her if he has done something she finds offensive.
• Get family counseling.
• Give her definite guidelines about how to act.
• Ask her to be as respectful of your husband as she is of other people.
• Ask her stepfather to think of a way to bridge the gap between them. Does he respect her?
• Listen to how she feels about your husband; then decide together what changes you, she, and he can make.
• Tell them both that you want and expect a change.
• Stay out of the middle of their relationship, unless either one asks for help.
• Read *Step Kids: A Survival Guide for Teenagers in Stepfamilies . . . and for Stepparents Doubtful of Their Own Survival* by Getzoff and McClenahan. (See **Resources**.)

Thanks to Jeannette Hickman-Kingsley, Circle from Minnetonka, Minnesota

D. Who Is in Charge of the Rules?

What is meant by natural and logical consequences?

- *Natural* consequences automatically follow a behavior. *Logical* consequences are related to the behavior and make sense to a person who is thinking clearly.

- Failing a course because she doesn't study is a *natural* consequence. Having to stay home on week nights to study is a *logical* consequence of the failure.

- Losing a friend because she's rude is *natural*. Writing a letter of apology to that friend is *logical*.

- In making contracts with our kids, we spell out the *logical* consequences we will impose if the contract is not kept.

- Missing lunch at school because she forgot to take the lunch you packed is *logical*. Being hungry because she missed lunch is *natural*.

- Feeling tired is the *natural* result of walking a long distance to school. Having to walk is the *logical* result of missing the school bus.

- Taking away television privileges for fighting at school is not logical. Having a problem-solving session with the child and school or insisting that the school enforce rules about fighting are *logical* consequences.

(See **Structuring for Independence and Responsibility**.)

Thanks to Mary Pannenen, Circle from Seattle, Washington

My thirteen-year-old wants to watch television all day. I want him to watch a few quality shows. What shall I do?

- Decide with him what is a reasonable amount of television time.
- Set your limits, then discuss with your son his choices within the limits.
- Have your son make a list of his favorite shows and then negotiate with him one quality show for each favorite show.
- Look at the TV schedule together. Negotiate limited time for TV, then discuss why he likes at least one program.
- Put an electric timer on the TV cord. Have your son set it for the one or two hours he wishes to watch.
- Talk to your son about why you want limits and how you feel about different programs.
- Have your son select priority programs and help him identify things to do instead of watching TV.
- Turn the TV to the wall for two weeks to break the daily habit. Then negotiate times and programs.
- Watch television with him. Help him develop critical viewing by discussing each show with him as soon as it is over.

(See also D-1.)

Thanks to Sandra Petty, Circle from Marshall, Michigan

My fifteen-year-old is on the phone all the time, usually in her room with the door closed and the stereo on. What should I do?

- Allow your teen to have privacy on the phone.
- Get a second phone or get "interrupt" service so calls can come in.
- Give her an egg-timer to watch. Four "three-minute eggs" per call!
- Set limits on the time of day when each person can use the phone.
- Encourage more personal meetings without the phone by recommending sports, other activities, or visits from friends.
- Let her pay for all or part of a phone of her own.
- Figure out together what the rules should be.
- Make a deal: For every half hour of private phone use, she is to give fifteen minutes of family participation in games, conversations, or sharing chores.
- Give a choice: the stereo or the phone, not both.

(See also D-1 and **Ages and Stages**.)

Thanks to Sara Monser, Circle from Pleasant Hill, California

My teens use language that is highly offensive. How can I stop this?

- Tell them your ears hurt and the prescribed treatment is to rest them from offensive language.
- Say, "Don't talk like that. I find your language highly offensive."
- Ask them to define the words they use.
- As you walk out of the room, tell them you will not subject yourself to that language.
- Say, "Powerful people don't need to use offensive or abrasive language. You can be powerful and think before you talk."
- Put your hands over your ears. Say "Stop."
- Ask them to look for ways the same feelings can be expressed without using offensive language.
- Fine them twenty-five cents a word. Then donate the money to the charity of their choice.
- Refuse to respond to any request that includes offensive language.
- Watch your own language.
- Tape the language. Ask if they are willing to listen to the tape and hear how they sound or if they prefer to stop talking that way in your presence.

(See also C-3, D-1.)

Thanks to Gail Davenport, Alderwood Manor, Washington

My teen's room is a constant mess, and he refuses to clean it when I ask him.

- Give him a choice: Clean the room and have his weekend free or stay home on the weekend until it is clean.
- Provide positive incentives for his keeping it clean.
- Together, figure out a written chart of jobs that includes a day for cleaning his room. Use a point and reward system of something he wants for maintaining it.
- Hire someone to clean his room and deduct the cost from his allowance.
- Show him how to clean a room quickly and efficiently so it's not such a big job.
- Trade jobs with him. You'll clean his room if he'll do one of your jobs.
- Help him plan an overnight party for his friends in his room.
- Look at his messy room as his problem, not yours.
- Think about what your concern is. Could it be what others might think, or is it concern about your child's lack of structure? If the concern is structure, contract with him to improve that.
- Give him responsibility for maintaining his own things and his own space.
- Close the door.

(See also A-1, D-1, and **Structuring for Independence and Responsibility**.)

Thanks to Harold Nordeman, Cincinnati, Ohio

When my teen challenges me with "I don't have to do what you say. It's my life. I can do what I want," I'm unsure how much freedom I should allow and how much I should protect her.

- Say, "It *is* your life *and* I expect you to live by certain values. Where specifically do you want more freedom?"
- Tell her it's OK to become separate, but she still can't do everything she wants.
- Discuss what might happen if each of us did only what we wanted.
- Check the rules to be sure they are appropriate for her age.
- Listen to find out if she wants more freedom or more clearness about what's important to you.
- Ask, "What is it you want to do? How will you handle the responsibility for that?"
- Stay open to your child's hopes, dreams, and rebellions, and set limits if her monologue doesn't allow for dialogue.
- Remember that teens often need to test for limits. Decide on your important limits and be firm about them.
- Sometime each day let her know that you love her.
- Say, "None of us can do only what we want. Follow the rules."
- Say, "It is important to learn to be cooperative as well as independent."

(See also D-1, E-1, and **Ages and Stages**.)

Thanks to Sara Monser, Lafayette, California

My husband's daughter bounces back and forth between our house and her mother's, because she won't abide by the rules in either household. What should I do?

- Get all adults involved to agree upon a set of rules to be enforced consistently in both households. Then carry them out.
- Point out to her that the alternative to living in her parents' homes is to live in a foster or group home.
- Develop with her a written contract listing benefits of living with you. Agree on rules of the household and consequences of breaking the rules.
- Insist that she think about how her actions are affecting the lives of others around her.
- Use the Yorks' *ToughLove* guidelines if the child needs a drastic change to get her attention. (See **Resources.**)
- Be sure you and your husband are clear and united in your approach to rules.
- Ask her to participate in setting household rules that are acceptable to you and help in establishing consequences.
- Keep rules as few and basic as possible to allow consistent enforcement.

(See also D-1, D-6, and **Structuring for Independence and Responsibility.**)

Thanks to Sara Monser, Circle from Lafayette, California

Our sixteen-year-old daughter smokes cigarettes. We disapprove. How do we set house rules and what rules can we set?

- Set a rule of no smoking in the house. Set consequences if she is caught smoking or if cigarettes are found in the house.
- Tell her if she must smoke, she must smoke outside.
- Say, "I am opposed to smoking. If you are going to smoke it must be outside of our house."
- Say, "Your body is important. Smoking is hard on it. I will not be a part of your smoking. You may not smoke in the house."
- Say, "Non-smokers inhale lots of smoke when others smoke. You may not damage my body by smoking in the house."
- Say, "In this state it is illegal to buy cigarettes at your age. No smoking until you are eighteen!"
- Post the rules and enforce them with penalties for breaking them such as grounding, fines, or removal of driving privileges.
- Be clear that you disapprove and that no smoking is allowed in the house.
- Model no smoking: if you smoke, stop.

(See also B-1, D-1, and E-3.)

Thanks to Julia Moen, Circle from Minneapolis, Minnesota

E. Peers, Friends, and Loves

How do I respond when my daughter says "Everyone is doing it"?

- Say, "*Everyone*???"
- Say, "You can set a precedent."
- Find out what specifically she wants to do and figure out if she can do it safely.
- Ask her to think of five other reasons to do it besides "Everyone is doing it" and then you'll discuss it with her.
- Ask her to look at all the beautiful ways she is not "everyone" and can decide for herself what is right for her.
- Tell a story of someone her age who didn't do what "everyone" did and was better for it.
- Give her the affirmations for structure. (See page 21.)
- Say, "I'm not sure about that. If you insist, I'll call six mothers of your friends and ask if their girls can do this."
- Check with her school counselor to find out how many are really doing it.
- Say, "I bet it seems that way. How many people do you count in 'everyone'?"
- Kids this age need to belong. Help her to belong and be unique at the same time.

(See also B-1, D-1, E-2, E-3, **Ages and Stages**, and **Structuring for Independence and Responsibility**.)

Thanks to Sara Monser, Circle from Lafayette, California

I don't like my son's friends. He's always out with them and I feel I don't have much influence on him anymore.

• Keep track of hours he is away and hours he's at home to see if he is gone excessively or if it just feels like it to you.
• Keep the refrigerator well stocked and you may see more of your son and his friends, too! Look for their positive points and comment on them.
• Support positive activities your son is interested in. Support these interests with your presence as well as your money, transportation, and time.
• Tell your child *why* you don't like his friends.
• Talk to his school counselor and teachers about the situation.
• Read *The One-Minute Father/Mother* by Spencer Johnson. (See **Resources**.)
• Ask your son to think about what his friends will probably be doing ten years from now and ask if that's what he wants for himself.
• Support what your son does well so he sees himself as worthwhile. Friends reflect a child's needs.
• Decide if this is your problem or your son's, since it is time for him to start separating from you. Are you ready to let him go?

(See also E-1, E-3, and **Ages and Stages**.)

Thanks to Harold Nordeman, Circle from Cincinnati, Ohio

My fifteen-year-old child's friends all smoke, and she feels immature when she refuses to smoke. How can I help her?

- Praise her for being mature enough to make her own choices.
- Stress the importance of being an individual in a world that is constantly attempting to get you to conform.
- Give her special privileges for her decision not to smoke.
- Use affirmations with her: "You can find a way of doing things that works for you." (See page 21.)
- Show her the research that supports the wisdom of her choice.
- Suggest she may be the person others imitate in time.
- Talk with her about what "mature" means; use her choice as an illustration of mature behavior.
- Hug her often when she hasn't been with her smoking friends and tell her how nice she smells.
- Wonder with her why people choose to smoke.
- Tell her to come and talk to you about it whenever she needs to.
- Compliment her on her mature ability to have friends who differ from her.
- Be clear about your no-smoking rule.

(See also D-8, **Ages and Stages**, and **Structuring for Independence and Responsibility**.)

Thanks to Judy Popp, Yakima, Washington

How do I get my teens to come home for snacks and further partying after dances and shows rather than going to a "joint" or parking?

• Tell them they are welcome to bring their friends home.

• Don't "hang out" with them when they come home. Greet them and then disappear without leaving the house.

• Have a refrigerator full of food and soft drinks.

• Offer videotapes, records, and games.

• Talk with their friends. Get to know them. Be friendly.

• Provide an affirming environment for teens by being friendly and giving them space in the house separate from the rest of the family.

• Cultivate an attitude that is inviting and makes clear that the kids are not a bother.

• Have the kids come over ahead of time to clean up and decorate for the party after the dance.

• Invite the group back the next day to return the house to its original condition.

• Figure out with your kids ways to make home after dates better than "joints" or parking.

• Look for ways to have fun with your teens much of the time so they prefer to come home where they feel good.

Thanks to Deane Gradous, Circle from St. Paul, Minnesota

My sixteen-year-old daughter has made arrangements to travel with her boyfriend to visit a prospective college that is seven hours away. I don't think it's a good idea for the two of them to drive that far and spend the night. What should I tell my daughter?

- Say, "We don't agree with the two of you going together. We will take you, and your boyfriend is welcome to come along."
- Suggest that you and your daughter go together.
- Reschedule the trip so that a parent or an older brother or sister can see the school and help with the driving.
- It's all right for you as her parent to say no.
- Discuss your concerns and find out how *she* views the trip. Let her know that you expect her to use good judgment.
- It is time to talk about next year's college, away-from-home rules, and how she plans to cope with pressures to have sex.
- Plan a trip with her so you all—parents, too—can see several colleges that she's interested in, all on one trip.

(See also B-9, B-12, D-1, and **Structuring for Independence and Responsibility**.)

Thanks to Sandy Keiser, Circle from Cincinnati, Ohio

Our teenager wants to get married so they can be together while they are in college. I think they are too young. What should I do?

- Since you think they are too young, say so and tell them why.
- Ask questions like "What will you do if you have a baby? How will you support yourselves? What about continuing your educations?"
- Figure out a way to help him without his entering into marriage.
- All involved have a session with a family counselor.
- If they are sexually active, see that they have accurate birth control information and access to the products through clinics or doctors.
- Accept their sexual desires and growing love, and talk with them about the commitment. Are they ready for that?
- Listen to their hopes and dreams and help them figure out the best way to achieve them.
- Explain that if they love each other their love will grow whether they are married or not.
- Let him know if you are willing to continue giving the same financial support, more or less, if he marries.
- Ask them to think what each of them will be like at thirty if they marry now or if they marry later.

(See also B-12, D-1, E-5, and **Ages and Stages**.)

Thanks to Gail Nordeman, Circle from Healdsburg, California

My eighteen-year-old wants to live with her boyfriend at college. How do I handle this?

- Thank her for talking with you about it. Tell her how you prefer that she behave and that you'll love her whatever she does.
- Consider that she may be asking you to say no. Otherwise she might not have asked.
- Say no and help her figure out how she can tell her friend no.
- If you have strong feelings against it, say no.
- Ask, "If you live together, which of you will be responsible for birth control?"
- Ask, "Why do you want to do this?" Discuss the options, then decide how to handle it.
- Remind her that she'll be setting an example for her younger siblings. She may want to know what happened with other couples to learn from their example, just as her sibs will learn from hers.
- Point out that this is an adult decision and, as such, means she must assume the other responsibilities of adulthood.
- Have her boyfriend in on the discussion about the pros and cons of the arrangement and share how you think and feel about it.

(See also B-12, B-13, D-1, E-6, and **Structuring for Independence and Responsibility**.)

Thanks to Sara Monser, Circle from Lafayette, California

F. Curfews and Cars and Chores

My fourteen-year-old daughter wants to stay out later than midnight. What shall I do?

- Say, "Yes, you may stay out past midnight. Your new curfew is 12:10. Not a *moment* past!"
- Each June when school is out, increase the time she can stay out.
- If you live in an area that has a curfew law, obey it.
- Have her call you when she gets to the party and finds out what the party is like. Then decide on a time you both think is appropriate.
- Evaluate each event and set the curfew accordingly.
- Tell her she can't.
- Ask her what time she plans to be in. Then compromise on an accepted time.
- Invite her to bring friends home if she wants to continue to party past midnight.
- Discuss with her a set of rules about curfews, based on events and peer groups, that is agreeable for both of you.
- Base curfew decisions on your child's overall demonstration of good judgment.
- Allow her to stay later at a friend's house if there are chaperones.

(See also A-2.)

Thanks to Harold Nordeman, Circle from Cincinnati, Ohio

82

I worry when my sixteen-year-old son is late. He apologizes and thinks that should end it. How can I let him know what I expect of him?

- Tell him, "I expect you to be here when you say you will be."
- Tell him you're concerned about him because you love him, and when he doesn't let you know when he's going to be late, you're afraid something has happened to him.
- Tell him, "I don't like being left without contact. If you will be more than a half hour late, call me and let me know where you are and what is happening."
- Say, "I expect you to provide (amount of) hours of fun with me to make up for the worrying I did."
- Look at your expectations to see if they are realistic. Then clarify curfews so there is no misunderstanding of expectations.
- The next time you are late, ask him how he feels. Think about whether this is a pattern for you and what effect it has on him.
- After you let him know what you expect, set consequences and carry them through, or it may not make any difference.
- Notice when he is on time or early. Praise him for the positive behavior.

(See also A-1, D-1, and D-6.)

Thanks to Sandra Sittko, Circle from St. Louis, Missouri

My daughter has no license and she drove a car. What shall I do?

• Say, "Stop! It's illegal to drive without a license. Call me when you need transportation."
• Say, "Wait until you have your license."
• Ground her for two weeks.
• Say, "I care about you. Don't do that again."
• Say, "You could end up in the slammer."
• Say, "You have done so many creditable things. This doesn't seem like you. What's going on?"
• Sign her up for driving lessons, and tell her she can drive when she gets a license.
• See that she gets a learner's permit. Then spend quality time with her refining her driving skills.
• Say, "Think of what happens to people who disobey the law."
• Spend a day with her observing traffic court.

(See also D-1, D-6, F-5, and **Structuring for Independence and Responsibility**.)

Thanks to Jean Clarke, Circle from Bloomington, Minnesota

The first day my son drove the family car, he was responsible for a minor accident that cost $2,000 for repairs. How do we make this into a positive lesson?

- Have him pay the deductible or at least a portion of it so he experiences the consequences of his behavior.
- $2,000 doesn't sound minor. Think this through again for yourself. You might be encouraging him to disregard the seriousness of this situation.
- Have him do the footwork of getting the estimates and insurance work completed. Be available to help him if he asks.
- Until the car is repaired, limit his use of other means of family transportation.
- Have him create options for family members who need transportation such as getting information about taxis, bus schedules, etc.
- Look at other areas of your child's life. If he is irresponsible in other areas, get help.
- Ask him, "How could you have avoided the accident?" Make contracts about his future driving.
- Ask him how he feels. Accept his feelings and urge him to turn the energy from his feelings into responsible action.
- Tell him you love him and that he is to drive safely.

Thanks to Sara Monser, Circle from Lafayette, California

How can I get teenagers to do kitchen duty?

- Tell them, "When you use dishes, put them in the washer."
- Suggest that they work as a team, helping each other out on days when doing the dishes is inconvenient.
- If dishwashing rules are clear, leave the dishes until they are done.
- Use the rules that they clean up their own dishes individually plus two cooking pots per person.
- If the assigned dishwasher does the dishes, then anyone finishing after that should do her own.
- See that the dishes are done before the assigned dishwasher can leave the kitchen.
- Ask kids to make out a schedule of kitchen jobs that is fairly balanced. Then encourage them to be responsible by enforcing consequences.
- Make a rule that dishes must be done sometime before those responsible go to bed. Enforce it with consequences.
- Call a family meeting for establishing a rotating schedule of household chores.
- Celebrate with sparklers in the dessert every week the kids have done their jobs without hassle.

(See also D-1, D-5, and **Structuring for Independence and Responsibility**.)

Thanks to Marilyn Grevstad, Circle from Seattle, Washington

I tell my fifteen-year-old son to do something at home and he doesn't do it. How can I get him to be more responsible?

- Tell him he is important to the family and you expect his help.
- Say clearly that a job is a job even if it is at home.
- Ask him, "What do you need to handle your responsibilities at home?"
- Ask him to look at why it is a problem, and tell him what you expect from him.
- List jobs he can do. State how many you expect him to do and tell him if he doesn't do these jobs, he can expect consequences. Then outline them.
- Decide what his reward is for completing his jobs on time.
- Allow him to experience consequences of his behavior that will inconvenience him, not you: No TV, no music, no access to the refrigerator, extra errands.
- If a job is supposed to be done at a certain time, be sure to enforce consequences for not meeting the deadline.
- Recognize when he is acting responsibly at home and compliment him.

(See also C-1, D-1, D-5, and **Structuring for Independence and Responsibility**.)

Thanks to Suzanne Morgan, Circle from Albert Lea, Minnesota

G. Identity and Self-Esteem

My son is short and stout and his classmates call him names and he feels different. How can I help?

- Take him to the doctor to find out if he's in the normal range. If he is, work on self-esteem. If not, help him find a diet.
- Say, "You can learn a lot about problem-solving from this situation. I'll support you."
- Point out role models from history of people who were different and succeeded.
- Teach him ways to ignore name calling or turn it into humor. Rehearse with him some clever (not hurting) responses that he can use when attacked. Get *Ouch, That Hurts!* by Clarke. (See **Resources**.)
- Help him learn good eating habits, but let him be in charge of any weight loss.
- Point out the child's strengths and abilities and focus on acceptance of himself rather than seeing himself as odd.
- Let him know that you love him the way he is. Have him identify ways other teenagers are different also.
- If he is overweight, offer to take him to a weight-loss group and provide wholesome food.
- Give him lots of Being messages. (See page 19.)

(See also G-2, G-3, G-4, G-5, and **Ages and Stages**.)

Thanks to Sara Monser, Circle from Lafayette, California

My daughter is sure there is something wrong with her, since she is still flat-chested at sixteen.

- Read a book together that shows pictures of different sizes and shapes. Talk about what's normal and OK. *Changing Bodies, Changing Lives* by Ruth Bell is a good one. (See **Resources**.)
- Ask her to notice all the different breast sizes when she is in the school locker room—not just the larger ones.
- Listen carefully to her worry. Your respect for her is important.
- Assure her that her body's way of maturing has its own time schedule, and her body may have breast development way down on the agenda.
- Look with her at your family's bodies. Maybe this is genetic.
- Once she is assured of her normalcy, offer to buy her a slightly padded bra if she is self-conscious.
- If she is not yet menstruating at sixteen, she should be evaluated by her physician.
- Point out some beautiful, outstanding women in our culture who happen also to be small breasted.
- Read *The Family Book About Sexuality* by Calderone and Johnson and then give it to your daughter to read. (See **Resources**.)

(See also G-1, G-3, G-4, and G-5.)

Thanks to Deane Gradous, Circle from Minneapolis, Minnesota

My teenager gets teased because he has zits. How can I help him handle the teasing?

- Tell him to say, "Hey, it's my meanness coming out. Be careful."
- Take him to see the movie *Mask*, which is about the elephant-man disease. The teenager in the movie handled being teased in several effective ways.
- Tell him to say, "Thank you," and change the subject.
- Tell him to smile and say, "Yes, it's a sign of raging hormones."
- Tell him how you felt and how you handled it.
- Tell him to say, "Yea, they are a problem. What did you use that worked?"
- Read *Ouch, That Hurts: A Handbook for People Who Hate Criticism* by Jean Illsley Clarke. (See **Resources**.)
- Tell him kids tease to cover their own insecurity and he doesn't have to take it seriously or respond.

Thanks to Mary Ann Lisk, Circle from Minnetonka, Minnesota

My junior-high teen is upset by the frequent use of the words *homo*, *queer*, *les*, and *gay* as name-calling. How can I help?

• Tell her that a personal attack like this is one way kids attempt to deal with their own questions about their sexuality.
• Let her know you care for her as she is and as she is becoming.
• You might tell her about your thoughts and feelings about sexuality when you were her age.
• Talk about homosexuality factually with her and offer to find a book to tell her more.
• Create opportunities to be available for her to talk with you.
• Ask her if she wants the help of a counselor.
• Ask her if she knows what a lesbian is and if her friends know or if they are just doing some name-calling.
• Tell her name-calling is serious because it attacks a whole group of people and that it is not OK behavior.
• Tell her it is important for kids her age to have close same sex friends, and it's your job as a parent to support her in those friendships because kids need to have those friendship bonds.

(See **Ages and Stages** and **Affirmations for Growth**)

Thanks to Ellen Peterson, Circle from Walnut Creek, California

Our teenage child feels so different from the rest of the family that he suspects he's adopted. I don't know how to reassure him.

- Tell him it's OK to be different and he *is* a part of the family.
- Be sure you love him for who he is and tell him so.
- If he is adopted, tell him so.
- Reassure him that you love him and ask him to talk with you if he needs help or feels lonely or left out.
- Tell him that as teenagers grow and separate, they sometimes feel this way and that, yes, he is your child.
- Show him his birth certificate or adoption papers. Tell him stories about his birth and infancy.
- Say, "What would help you feel better about being in our family?"
- Help him see his differences as special and wonderful, to be treasured by him just as you treasure his uniqueness.
- Perhaps he marches to a different drummer. Point out ways diversity enriches the family.
- If the family is doing some "You are OK only if you are stamped in the family mold," change that.

(See also C-12 and **Affirmations for Growth**.)

Thanks to Christine Ternand, Circle from St. Paul, Minnesota

I would like suggested responses for my daughter, who wants me to feel sorry for her.

- Have her describe situations in which she used her power to effect a positive outcome. Ask her to think how she can use those qualities in this situation.
- Say, "I can't make your decisions for you, but I'm glad to be a sounding board."
- Contract for five minutes to play "Oh Poor Me" or "Ain't It Awful" games for fun to help her get it out of her system so she can problem solve.
- Help her break the problem down into pieces and set priorities.
- Give her lots of hugs and Being messages. (See page 19.)
- Say, "I won't feel sorry for you. I *will* love you and think with you. If you want specific help from me, please ask."
- Say, "You are a powerful person. You can decide how you will resolve that situation."
- Say, "You have a lot to think about. I trust you to think clearly. Let me know how I can help you."
- Together list ten possible solutions to the situation. Include funny and ridiculous ideas as well as serious and thoughtful ones.
- Encourage her to separate facts from opinions and judgments. Ask her what you can do that would invite her to feel better about herself.

Thanks to Sue Hansen, Circle from Bellevue, Washington

H. Values and Idealism

My junior-high child came home with seventy-dollar jeans he had got on sale for fifty dollars, and I had a fit. He couldn't understand why. He will outgrow them in a month. Help!

- Compliment him for finding a bargain. Then discuss the total amount to be spent on his clothes this year.
- Give him a clothing allowance on a weekly basis so he will have to save it up to get expensive jeans.
- Let him dress the way the other kids do if he can pay for the clothes.
- Think of this as an opportunity for you to teach him values.
- Ask him to keep track of how fast he is growing and figure out how often he will need new clothes while he grows this fast.
- Go shopping with him and teach him how to buy within a budget.
- Think if you have spent fifty dollars on clothes for him for a special occasion. Ask yourself if this is different.
- If you have him on a clothing allowance, this is his problem and his learning experience.
- If your family can't afford this type of expenditure, tell him so and show him where the money is needed.

(See also D-1.)

Thanks to Carole Gesme, Circle from Minneapolis, Minnesota

Our daughter's friends are getting expensive gifts for graduation, but we don't feel we can afford an expensive gift for her. What should I do?

• Do what your values and purse dictate.

• Explain to her, "I'll be extravagant with love for you and do the best I can with monetary gifts."

• Tell her how proud you are of her achievement and give her the gift you can afford without apology.

• Suggest that you can come up with X dollars for what she wants, if she can come up with the rest.

• If she wants a special gift, explore with her why the gift is so important.

• Go on a fantasy shopping spree together and share all the things you wish you could have or buy if you had unlimited funds.

• Discuss with her your whole value system—how you feel about money and how it is used.

• If you have one, give her a family heirloom or other sentimental gift.

• Offer a special gift, like a picture album or a growing-up ritual, without spending much money.

Thanks to Jean Clarke, Circle from Minneapolis, Minnesota

How do we teach our adolescents good manners like thank you letters and consideration of others?

- Provide personalized note paper and stamps. Tell them to use it to write thank you notes.
- Show them a sample thank you note to use as a model.
- Decide if your standards are realistic for your kids' ages and situation. Be consistent in your expectations.
- Evaluate your respect and courtesy toward them, for they will learn from you how to act toward others.
- Point out specific behaviors you don't like. Make suggestions for things to do instead.
- Compliment them for the positive manners they do have.
- Let them know how good manners can ease the path for them.
- Get a good etiquette book as a gift for them.
- Talk with them about how important the consideration you receive from friends is for you.
- Occasionally "invite" your teens to be "guests" at family dinner. On other occasions, ask them to "host" a family meal. Have fun and later discuss manners that may need improving— perhaps some of your own.
- Model what you want: Allow them to overhear you comment positively when you receive a thank you note.

Thanks to Harold Nordeman, Circle from Cincinnati, Ohio

Our son refuses to go to church with us. We believe religion is important. What can I do?

- Tell him he must go to church while he is living at home. When he's on his own, he may choose to go or not.
- Say, "You can skip church for three months. Then we will ask you to go for a month and see how it is."
- Ask him if he'd rather go to church with his friends and/or sit in a pew separate from you.
- Ask your son to investigate churches and find one he would choose to attend. Then support his choice.
- Discuss with him when this decision will be his to make and what you expect until that time.
- See your clergy to see if they will establish a program for teens that will fulfill their needs.
- If he says he is upset at the difference in adult behavior in church and out of church, remind him that we go to church to find ways to be better.
- If he doesn't know much about your religion, say, "We think you will need to know about your religious background. You may believe or not, but you must attend three events a month. You choose which ones."

(See also **Ages and Stages** and **Parents Get Another Chance—Recycling.**)

Thanks to Becky Monson, Circle from Minnetonka, Minnesota

The threat of nuclear war scares our teenagers. They feel angry and depressed and feel it is useless to work for their values. What can I do?

- Help them organize a group of friends and decide on some positive action, like a letter-writing or door-to-door awareness campaign.
- Figure out with them ways to be part of peace-promoting organizations.
- Include them in family decision-making and affirm their abilities to make a difference with their participation.
- Point out to them that the threat began in 1946. Anti-nuclear activity has had a significant success rate, so get involved.
- Model hope for your children. Fear is paralyzing; hope is energizing.
- Look for books that reflect hope rather than doom and all of you read them together.
- Write your representative in Congress for more information about what the government is doing to diminish the threat of war.
- Tell your children that their activity may actually make the difference.
- Become involved in peace-promoting activities yourself.
- Get *The Peace Catalogue* by Duane Sweeney. Read and share it with your kids. (See **Resources.**)

(See also I-4.)

Thanks to Sara Monser, Circle from Lafayette, California

I. Jobs, Leaving Home, the Future

My teen accepted a job without getting hours and pay clearly established. What can I do?

- Say, "Tell your supervisor that you didn't understand the hours and salary and that you need to go over the details again."
- Ask if she wants your help in solving this problem.
- Ask, "What do you think will happen if you continue to work without being sure what the hours and pay are?"
- Look with her at some ways she can get the information she needs. Do not offer to get the information for her.
- Say, "Talk to friends about the pay and conditions of their jobs. Then talk to your boss."
- Compliment her for getting a job and talk over what she plans to do next.
- Tell her a story about a similar problem from your past that includes how you solved the problem.
- Say, "I'm confident you will figure out what to do about this situation and that you'll ask for help if you need it."
- Ask an older sibling to share experiences about jobs with your daughter.
- If she is often irresponsible, don't do or say anything. Let her learn from the marketplace.

(See also D-1, I-2, and **Structuring for Independence and Responsibility**.)

Thanks to Melanie Weiss, Circle from Bellevue, Washington

My nineteen-year-old goes from job to job, never staying with one for more than a month or so. I'm worried how this will affect his future. What should I do?

- Find out why he is leaving his jobs. Is it because he can't get along with employers, has unrealistic expectations of the job, or what?
- Discuss with him the pattern of going from job to job and your fear that this pattern is a serious problem.
- Reduce your financial support so he has to work in order to have the things he wants.
- Evaluate what's happening at home. How much support for working does he get?
- Clarify with him his goal for working.
- Review the pattern to see if it's a pattern in his whole life, like going from friend to friend, school to school, or plan to plan for the future. If so, get counseling for him.
- Encourage him to stay with his current job for a period of time (six months) and say that you will help him work out any problem he is having there.
- If he has never worked before, don't worry if he explores jobs for the first four or five months.
- Could the problem be connected with drug abuse?

(See also B-5, D 1, and I-1.)

Thanks to Sara Monser, Circle from Lafayette, California

My daughter is in her first year at college and has been there three months. She is saying, "I want to come home. I want to quit college. I don't know what I want." What should I do?

- Ask her if she can stick it out and do her best until the end of the semester before deciding the next step.
- See if she is willing to study for a week, then call you to tell you how she is doing.
- Ask her how she is feeling physically. Suggest a consultation at the health center.
- Tell her you love her and wish you could hug her until she felt better just as you did when she was little, and then send brownies.
- Tell her to talk to her housemother, advisor, counselor, pastor, or friend and get extra help and support through the crisis.
- Ask her what she *will* do if she doesn't stay in school.
- Help her identify her areas of discomfort— school work, social and dates or girlfriend problems, or the homesickness. Then ask her to decide on and rate which are most important and in need of attention.
- Find out how else she needs you to help with homesickness, other than coming home.

(See also **Ages and Stages** and **Affirmations for Growth**.)

Thanks to Deane Gradous, Circle from Minneapolis, Minnesota

What do I say or do when my teenagers say, "I have no future; there is no future for me"?

- Say, "I believe you have a future, and I care about you."
- Listen to the ways they are afraid. If this is about the threat of nuclear war, figure out something you can do together to promote peace. Get *The Peace Catalogue* by Duane Sweeney. (See **Resources**.)
- Tell stories of times when you felt the same way and how you handled it.
- Ask if they mean personal competence, jobs, ecology, war, or whatever, and then brainstorm for options.
- Help them develop affirmations to say to themselves. (See page 000.)
- Say, "How can I help you?"
- Mention counseling as a possible way to deal with these feelings.
- Find out in a sensitive way if this is a suicidal cry for help. If it is, get help immediately.
- Tell them that a strong religious faith can help with this problem.
- Find out what they are feeling helpless about. Ask, "What do you mean?" Listen. Say, "I love you."
- Check for drug abuse.

(See also H-5.)

Thanks to Jean Clarke, Circle from Plymouth, Minnesota

Our teenager wants to join the Peace Corps after high school and skip college. What should I do?

• Encourage her to go for it.
• See this as possibly the best education she can get right now. Ask her to give you her time schedule for fulfilling her goal.
• Talk to her about taking a year or two of college first so she will be more valuable in the Peace Corps job.
• Ask her to talk to a school counselor and let you know what advice she gets.
• Encourage her to get involved in community activities as a volunteer for a summer; then review the Peace Corps option.
• Go as a family to an informational seminar on the Peace Corps to alleviate your fears.
• Say, "We love you and trust you to make good decisions about your life."
• Since the Peace Corps prefers experienced people, be prepared for the possibility of other nonacademic options.
• Ask her to finish college first.
• Ask her to go to college when she comes back.
• Be proud that you have raised such a caring, courageous daughter.
• Trust her.

(See also **Ages and Stages** and **Parents Get Another Chance—Recycling**.)

Thanks to Harold Nordeman, Circle from Cincinnati, Ohio

J. Parents Have Problems, Too

What can I do to raise my own self-esteem?

• Take a break. Sing a song. Take a bath. Take a fantasy trip. Change clothes.

• Schedule cheerleading sessions for yourself and ask other people to cheer for you also.

• Think about how you can live by these three guidelines: Love myself unequivocally; love others generously; be responsible for my part and my part only.

• Spend time with people who affirm you. Avoid those who depreciate you. (See page 18.)

• Work out of doors alone or with someone. Go for a long walk and concentrate on the beauty.

• Accept the fact that sometimes people feel low. Let it happen. Think what you can do to make those situations different next time.

• Keep notes and letters that are complimentary. Read them often.

• Learn a new skill and enjoy it.

• Write down twenty-two positive adjectives that describe you. Post them on your bathroom mirror and refrigerator door.

• Join a group that interests you and volunteer for a job you like.

• Read Clarke's *Self-Esteem: A Family Affair.* (See **Resources**.)

(See also **Parents Get Another Chance— Recycling**.)

Thanks to Sue Hansen, Circle from Bellevue, Washington

I want to know how to respond to those who say to me, "Don't rock the boat. Don't grow; don't change."

- Say, "I'm a natural, growing person."
- Sing the song, "I Gotta Be Me."
- Say, "It's OK for me to learn and grow."
- Tell them you will continue to care about them as you grow and change.
- Ask them to watch what happens when you grow and change. They may decide to try it!
- Say, "I hear your concerns, but it's too painful for me to stay this way."
- Say, "You may like me even better!"
- Say nothing. Hug them.
- Say, "Do you want to see me atrophy right here in front of you?"
- Say, "Too late. I've already started," with lightness in your voice.
- Tell them that adults have developmental tasks to do and that you are an adult. (See page 23.)

(See also **Parents Get Another Chance— Recycling**.)

Thanks to Lois White, Circle from Plymouth, Minnesota

My teenage child considers me an embarrassment. What do I do?

- Keep a sense of humor. Don't be hurt by his separating.
- Listen carefully to his feelings. Do not be defensive. Consider what he says and look at how you may contribute to his embarrassment.
- Be consistent in your behavior with your child. Tell him what he can expect of you in different situations.
- Acknowledge his discomfort and state, "It is appropriate for me to be here, doing this" (if it is).
- Discuss what he expects of you before situations in which he might feel embarrassed.
- Clean up your act. If your child is embarrassed because of inappropriate behavior (dressed in robe in front of friends, too much alcohol, etc.), *change*.
- If you are willing to change your behavior, go along with him.
- Avoid scolding or other inappropriate behavior in front of his friends.
- Remember that many teenagers feel this way no matter what their parents do.
- *Do* insist he continue to participate in important family functions. *Do not* expect to go to the movies with him on Friday night.

(See also C-6 and **Ages and Stages**.)

Thanks to Sara Monser, Lafayette, California

How can I communicate with my fourteen-year-old without losing my temper when she is going out and won't tell me where?

- Practice in front of a mirror saying calmly, "You can't go until you tell me where you are going."
- Tell her, "Your safety is important to me, and I need to know."
- When you are both calm, brainstorm with her about how to improve communication.
- Tell her to wait five minutes. Go in the bedroom and hit the pillow. Then, when you're calm, talk to her.
- Take a deep breath, speak slowly, and tell her what you want from her.
- Ask your spouse to take over for a few minutes while you breathe deeply and center yourself.
- During a time when you both are feeling good, discuss with her the responsibility that goes with living in a family, which includes letting each other know where we go.
- Ask her to call and tell you where she is when she gets there.
- Tell her why you are angry and ask her to help.
- If, underneath the anger, you are scared, tell her that.
- Be sure you tell her where you are going.

(See also C-1 and **Parents Get Another Chance— Recycling**.)

Thanks to Carole Gesme, Circle from Wayzata, Minnesota

I'm afraid to say no to my teenager, because he will break the furniture or hit me. What can I do?

- Tell him if he ever threatens you or strikes you again, you will call the police, and do it.
- Say, "Hitting is not allowed in this home. Do not ever threaten me with violence."
- Say a *firm* "Don't" from a this-is-the-way-it-is position.
- Tell him six ways that he can let out his anger that do not threaten you, such as yell (not at you), run, play tennis, hit the bean bag chair, etc.
- Both of you get into counseling in a hurry.
- Find out if he is abusing drugs.
- If you or your spouse break furniture or hit people, do whatever you need to do to stop that.
- Affirm yourself as a parent and your right to say no and set limits without being hurt.
- Review your rules and reconfirm the ones you've decided are important to enforce. Tell your child, when he is calm, that you will be doing that and that he must follow them if he is to continue living in your house. Investigate counseling and foster care.
- See a counselor and get some help with your fear and the lack of structure in your house.

(See also B-5, D-1, and **Where to Go for Additional Support**.)

Thanks to Carole Gesme, Circle from Minneapolis, Minnesota

How do we tell our teenagers that we are getting a divorce?

• Have a family meeting with everyone there. Make sure both parents take part in telling the children.

• Agree ahead of time that you will not put each other down in front of the children.

• When you tell them be sure and talk about what will happen to them: where they will live and how each of you will continue to parent.

• Be available to the children after you tell them of your decision, so they can come and talk.

• Take your time. You don't have to tell all the reasons when first talking about the divorce.

• Go to a family counselor with your family for support during this time.

• Both of you say, "I love you and even though your (mother/father) and I have decided to divorce, we will both be your parents and care for you. It is not your fault."

• Ask your spiritual leader for advice, support, and help during this time.

• Read the Duncans' *You're Divorced, But Your Children Aren't* or Jewett's *Helping Children Cope with Separation and Loss*. (See **Resources**.)

(See also **Where to Go for Additional Support**.)

Thanks to Gail Nordeman, Circle from Cincinnati, Ohio

This is my third marriage, and there are children from each, all teenagers. When we are together, how do I deal with their accusations of "favoritism"?

- Let them take turns choosing how the time will be spent.
- Set up a schedule that will allow special time for each child.
- Tell them you are glad to see each of them wanting attention and that you will be glad when they find a way to let you know without accusations.
- When a child says, "You like him better!" you say, "I care about you. Is there something special you need from me today?"
- Suggest, "You each fill up a different part of my heart. Right now, my left auricle needs attention, and that is your part."
- Have teens separate wants from needs. They may "want" to be king of the hill; they "need" love, supports, limits, and the space to separate.
- Say, "It's OK for you to compete in activities. You don't have to compete for my love."
- Give recognition for individual talents and achievements.
- If the accusation is true, admit it and change.
- Read *How to Win As a Stepfamily* by the Vishers.

(See also C-7, **Ages and Stages**, and **Affirmations for Growth**.)

Thanks to Linda Buranen, Minneapolis, Minnesota

**My stepdaughter feels she must lie to her mother
in order to stay her full visiting time with her dad.
How do I teach her to be honest, while protecting
her right to visit us?**

- Identify this as a problem the parents must solve
  and get the child out of the middle.
- Discuss with her when it is appropriate to lie,
  that is, when alone in the house, etc.
- Protecting visitation rights is up to your husband
  and his daughter. You get out of the middle.
- Insist that your husband get his ex-wife to
  adhere to the terms of the contract about visiting
  rights.
- Occasionally, go away from the house for the
  whole time of visitation. Leave it to them.
- Be consistently honest yourself so the child can
  see the advantages.
- Natural parents should work out this issue with
  attorneys or a counselor.
- Allow your stepchild to handle the situation as
  she sees she must, and discuss honesty versus
  expediency.
- Make sure the adults do the communicating
  about visitation so that the child doesn't have to
  lie.
- Offer love and stay out.

(See also **Affirmations for Growth**.)

Thanks to Sara Monser, Concord, California

•

I am a single parent. I work full time and travel some. How can I be a full-time parent to my fifteen-year-old son?

• Make a big calendar with your schedule and his. Then compare schedules once a week and make dates for special time together.
• Talk with your son about how the two of you can work together to solve the problem.
• Arrange a car pool for getting him to his activities. Find other parents who will help out.
• Use a tape recorder for messages to each other.
• Find some substitute parents for him while you are gone.
• Find people he can phone for support and structure while you are gone.
• Call Big Brothers, Kinship, or other organizations that match boys with caring adult men.
• Set an hour aside each week just for talking about how each of your lives is going.
• Include him as much as you can in the planning and arranging of his life.
• Ask his grandparents to help.
• Call home often.

(See also **Ages and Stages** and **Parents Get Another Chance—Recycling**.)

Thanks to Linda Buranen, Circle from Edina, Minnesota

Four Ways Young People Leave Home

One of the tasks of adolescents is to separate from parents in preparation for becoming independent.

Some teens separate pleasantly or with excitement and anticipation. Others act angry, as if the people they are separating from are despicable, disgusting, or at least terribly boring.

- The first way of separating is to *Leave*. It is used by the teen who leaves home in either a calm or angry way, is gone for some time, and then comes home and functions as a responsible adult in the extended family. He may then live at home or someplace else.

- The second way of separating is *Out and Back*. This child leaves home for a while, then is back home, then lives with friends for a few months, then moves home again. He repeats this process several times. Each time he comes home he is more self-sufficient and more responsible. This process of separation is completed when the young person is living at home or someplace else and is functioning as an equal adult in the world, not as a financially or emotionally dependent child.

- The third way of separating is to *Stay at Home*. The teen remains at home and becomes a financially responsible, emotionally differentiated adult.

- To be *Ejected* by the family is the fourth way of separating. The child who chooses this way uses family energy to help him move. He does whatever it takes to get the family to say firmly, "Sorry, you can't live here and do that." The child leaves and the separation is complete when the child has become a full, responsible adult in the community and in the extended family system. This is not to be confused with "kicking a child out" with threats and criticism that leave deep scars on both parents and adolescents.

Any of these four ways can result in successful separations. Sometimes parents and teens experience unnecessary stress when teens choose to separate in a way that is different from the one parents expect or the one they used.

—Jean Illsley Clarke

Where to Go for Additional Support

If you have talked with your family and friends, tried the ideas in the *HELP!* book, and still feel stuck with a problem, here are some places to call for additional help or for parenting classes. If you have difficulty finding a phone number after looking in both the white and the yellow pages, call any of these sources and ask them to help you find the number you need.

Community Services

Crisis or hot-line numbers
YMCA, YWCA, or a local church or synagogue
Chemical abuse treatment centers
Chemical abuse prevention programs
Community civic centers
Women's or men's support groups
Battered women's and children's shelters
Big Brothers/Big Sisters
Local hospitals
Alcoholics Anonymous
Parents Anonymous
Al-Anon
MADD
SADD

Schools

Community education (local school district)
Colleges or universities

Community colleges
Vocational and technical schools

Government

Community mental health
Public health nurse or department
Child protection services
Family service agencies
County social service agencies

Private Services

Psychologists, social workers, psychiatrists, therapists, family counselors

Interview the persons who will help you to see if they know about the area in which you need help. If don't get the help you need, go somewhere else until you do.

—The Editors

How to Lead a Suggestion Circle

The person leading the circle will do the following:

1. Ask people to sit in a circle.
2. Ask a member of the group to write down the suggestions for the person asking for help.
3. Ask people to respond to the question with their best suggestion and stop them if they ramble.
4. Go around the circle in order.
5. Ask people *not* to comment on each other's responses and interrupt them if they do.
6. Offer people the right to pass without being challenged.

The person asking for a Suggestion Circle will do this:

1. State the problem in a clear, short statement.
2. Respond to each member's suggestion with a "thank you."
3. Go home and think and act.

The group members will either respond with one short, quality answer, or pass. A group of twelve people can respond to a problem in about five minutes.

—Harold Nordeman

Resources

Bell, Ruth. *Changing Bodies, Changing Lives*. New York: Random House, 1980.

Bell, Ruth, and Zeiger, Leni. *Talking with Your Teenager: A Book for Parents*. New York: Random House, 1983.

Black, Claudia. *It Will Never Happen to Me!* Colorado Springs, Colo.: M.A.C. Printing and Publications Division, 1982.

The Boston Women's Health Book Collective. *Our Bodies, Ourselves*. Rev. ed. New York: Simon & Schuster, 1984.

Bayard, Robert T., and Bayard, Jean. *How to Deal with Your Acting-Up Teenager*. New York: M. Evans and Co., 1983.

Bradley, Buff. *Where Do I Belong? A Kids' Guide to Stepfamilies*. Reading, Mass.: Addison-Wesley, 1982.

Calderone, Mary S., and Johnson, Eric W. *The Family Book About Sexuality*. New York: Harper & Row, 1981.

Clark, Aminah, Clemes, Harris, and Bean, Reynold. *How to Raise Teenagers' Self-Esteem*. San Jose, Calif.: Enrich Division/OHAUS, 1983.

Clarke, Jean Illsley. *Self-Esteem: A Family Affair*. Minneapolis: Winston Press, 1978.

————. *Ouch, That Hurts! A Handbook for People Who Hate Criticism*. Plymouth, Minn.: Daisy Press, 1983.

Comfort, Alex, and Comfort, Jane. *The Facts of Love: Living, Loving and Growing Up*. New York: Ballantine Books, 1980.

Cretcher, Dorothy. *Steering Clear: Helping Your Child Through the High-Risk Drug Years*. Minneapolis: Winston Press, 1982.

Donlan, Joan. *I Never Saw the Sun Rise*. Minneapolis: CompCare Publications, 1977.

Duncan, T. Roger, and Duncan, Darlene. *You're Divorced, But Your Children Aren't*. Englewood Cliffs, N.J.: Prentice-Hall, 1979.

DuPont, Robert J., Jr. *Getting Tough on Gateway Drugs: A Guide for the Family*. Washington, D.C.: American Psychiatric Press, 1984.

Elkind, David. *All Grown Up and No Place to Go*. Reading, Mass.: Addison-Wesley, 1984.

———. *The Hurried Child: Growing Up Too Fast, Too Soon*. Reading, Mass.: Addison-Wesley, 1981.

Fahlberg, Vera. *Attachment and Separation*. Michigan Department of Social Sciences, 1979.

Getzoff, Ann, and McClenahan, Carolyn. *Step Kids: A Survival Guide for Teenagers in Stepfamilies . . . . and for Stepparents Doubtful of Their Own Survival*. New York: Warner Books, 1984.

Jewett, Claudia L. *Helping Children Cope with Separation and Loss*. Cambridge, Mass.: Harvard Common Press, 1982.

Johnson, Spencer. *The One-Minute Father/Mother*. New York: William Morrow, 1983.

Levenkron, Steven. *The Best Little Girl in the World*. Chicago: Contemporary Books, 1978.

Levin, Pamela. *Becoming the Way We Are*. Wenatchee, Wash.: Directed Media, Inc., 1974.

Lewis-Steere, Cynthia. *Stepping Lightly*. Minneapolis: CompCare Publications, 1981.

Little, Bill. *This Will Drive You Sane*. Minneapolis: CompCare Publications, 1980.

Madaras, Lynda, and Madaras, Area. *What's Happening to My Body? A Growing Guide for Mothers and Daughters*. New York: Newmarket Press, 1983.

Madaras, Lynda, and Saavedra, Dane. *What's Happening to My Body? A Book for My Boys*. New York: Newmarket Press, 1984.

May, Rollo. *Power and Innocence: A Search for the Sources of Violence*. New York: W. W. Norton, 1972.

Mayle, Peter. *What's Happening to Me?* Secaucus, N.J.: Lyle Stuart, 1975.

McCoy, Kathy, and Wibbelsman, Charles. *Teenage Body Book*. New York: Simon & Schuster, 1984.

McEvoy, Alan W., and Brookings, Jeff B. *If She Is Raped*. Holmes Beach, Fla.: Learning Publications, 1984.

National Institute on Drug Abuse. *Parents: What Can You Do About Drug Abuse?* Prevention Branch, Room 11A-43, 5600 Fishers Lane, Rockville, Md. 20857.

Nelson, Gerald E. *The One-Minute Scolding*. Boulder, Colo.: Shambhala Publications, 1984.

Otteson, Orlo, and Townsend, John. *Kids and Drugs: A Parent's Guide*. New York: CFF Publishing Corp., 1983.

Polson, Beth, and Newton, Miller. *Not My Kid: A Parent's Guide to Kids and Drugs*. New York: Avon, 1984.

Sanford, Linda. *The Silent Children*. New York: Doubleday, 1980.

Stoltz, Sandra Gordon. *The Food Fix*. Englewood Cliffs, N.J.: Prentice-Hall, 1983.

Sweeney, Duane. *The Peace Catalogue: A Guidebook to a Positive Future*. Seattle: Press for Peace, 1984.

Typpo, Marion H., and Hastings, Jill M. *An Elephant in the Living Room*. Minneapolis: CompCare Publications, 1984.

Visher, John, and Visher, Emily. *How to Win As a Stepfamily*. Chicago: Contemporary Books, 1982.

York, Phyllis, and York, David. *ToughLove*. Sellersville, Penn.: Community Service Foundation, 1980.

About the Editors

Jean Illsley Clarke is the author of the book *Self-Esteem: A Family Affair* and of the parenting program of the same name. The Suggestion Circle technique comes from that program. Jean is a Transactional Analyst, a parent educator, and a mother of three. She holds a Master of Arts in Human Development and an honorary Doctor of Human Services. She likes being with teenagers and parents of teenagers.

Sara Monser and her husband, Carl, have four young adult children. Sara holds a master's degree in educational psychology. In addition to teaching child and adolescent development and parenting skills classes at Diablo Valley Community College in Pleasant Hill, California, she coordinates the foster parent education program for the college and serves on community boards and committees which focus on enhancing adolescent self-esteem and on the prevention of abuse.

Gail Nordeman, R.N., B.A., **and Harold Nordeman** have parented five teenagers and are the founders and directors of "A Growing Place," an educational, counseling, and consulting center in Cincinnati, Ohio. They have taught preadolescence sex education classes, "Self-Esteem: A Family Affair" workshops, and have coauthored "Affirmations for Adult Children of Alcoholics." Gail is a registered nurse with clinical provisional teaching membership in the International Transactional Analysis Association. Harold is a personal communication consultant and author of "The Suggestion Circle as a Therapeutic Tool."

Index

131

Other Learning Materials Available

Developmental Tapes, by Jean Illsley Clarke. These audio cassette tapes present important information about children and the nurturing they need. Told in entertaining and easy-to-understand language from the perspective of children of different ages, the tapes describe child care by parents and by day-care providers. The stories allow adults to set aside fear or guilt and have the distance they may need to hear the information presented. The tapes, told in both male and female voices, are also useful tools for helping older children understand their little brother's and sister's needs and behavior. Each story is twelve-to-eighteen minutes long; at least eight spaced listenings are recommended.

Ups and Downs with Feelings, by Carole Gesme. This collection of games features a game board with a wide variety of "feeling faces" to help children and adults identify feelings and learn ways to be responsible for them. Included are directions for seven separate games, one of which uses the affirmations printed in this book.

Affirmation Cards. Tiny colored cards, with a separate affirmation printed on each, that can be read, carried, or given as gifts.

For more information, including prices, write to

Daisy Press
16535 Ninth Avenue North
Plymouth, MN 55447